Cracking Black & Blue

Aliza T. Speaks

Amelia!
Thank you for
supporting my
first novel :) I
really appreciate the
support. It has been
a pleasure attending
FLETC with you. Hope to
visit your city soon.
♡ Aliza T.

Cover Design by Monique Johnson

Author Photo by Timothy Bowser Multimedia, LLC

Aliza Speaks, LLC
P. O. Box 971
Kernersville, NC, 27285

www.alizatspeaks.com

ISBN: 978-0-9995781-6-2

DEDICATION

This book is dedicated to my father, heaven's angel.

June 17th, 1959 -September 30th, 1994

CONTENTS

	The Prelude	iii
1	The Struggle is Real	1
2	Conditional Offer Please	Pg 16
3	Recruits on Your Feet!!	Pg 31
4	Field Training	Pg 51
5	Misses Officer	Pg 68
6	Use of Force	Pg 85
7	Hands Up, Don't Shoot	Pg 98
8	Twelve	Pg 108
9	Robocops	Pg 122
10	The Come Up	Pg 137
11	Detective Singleton	Pg 149
12	Cracked Black & Blue	Pg 159

ACKNOWLEDGMENTS

Heavenly Father, thank you for fueling my steps with passion to address tensions between police and communities throughout America. I know that you are using me as a vessel to Speak. To my editors Tamriage Martin, Dr. L. R. Walker, and Desiree Montgomery thank you for all your help. Tamriage I appreciate the countless hours you spent reading my book. Your combination of criticism followed up with "positive vibes" was heart-warming. Dr. L. R. Walker not only did you handle your role as Consulting Editor with ease, you continuously inspired me throughout this journey. My sorority sister, Desiree Montgomery you were the first to review my work and encourage the dream. A tie for the listening ear award goes to my grandmother and Khaila Martin. Shout out to my mother, the MOM-A-GER, for your continued wisdom. Thanks to the Creator for giving me an invaluable team to which I shall be forever indebted.

THE PRELUDE

The spring commencement promptly begins at Minor Hills Agricultural & Technical State University, not on colored people time. A young twenty-three-year-old woman sat patiently for her name to be called, excited the Lord had seen fit to order her steps this far. She was thinking about an uneasy childhood and how she was never supposed to amount to anything. The constant reminders of her inadequacies were just the devil's attempt to break her spirit. "You are not going to be shit! What man is ever going to want you? You are going to be fifteen and pregnant!" The bashing continued like a song on repeat. These demeaning words came from her stepfather Braxton, a rebound for her mother.

To be frank, he was a reject. Braxton was a pretty boy with dirty habits; alcoholic, womanizer, and a down low brother working at the local factory. The young woman's mother, Agni was a math teacher at the local high school. Agni had a burning passion to improve academic achievement for her fully capable, yet economically disadvantaged students. Such devotion led to Agni being named

"Teacher of the Year," a prestigious accolade that many in her profession could only dream of. Prior to Agni's hire, the school had the lowest test scores in the district. In seemingly no time, her students not only had the highest test scores in Geometry for the district, but also the state. Teaching came naturally to Agni with her mellow and easy-going personality. Nonetheless, she still had her weaknesses. Those weaknesses led her right into the arms of "fuckboy" Braxton. From the outside looking in, Agni's divorce from Reverend Singleton was the catalyst. See, Reverend Singleton and Agni grew up together in the church as friends. Agni was a cheerleader in college, while Reverend Singleton was associate pastor of Mt. Zion Baptist Church. He wooed Agni off her feet with daily carnations to symbolize his admiration and love. And as any good fairytale goes, "first came love, then came marriage." Unfortunately, wedded bliss was short-lived, as Reverend Singleton learned his battle with sickle-cell anemia would shortly be coming to an end. Overwhelmed, he withdrew and became distant, letting go of the woman he loved.

However, during their short marriage Agni and Reverend Singleton did do one thing right. They created a beautiful child now sitting at commencement awaiting the announcer's call of her name at North Carolina's most revered historically black university. While her mind was wandering anxiety began to set in as she heard them stumbling over her friend "Quincyanna Taylor Smith's" name. She thought to herself, "What if I trip and fall? Even worse...What if I trip, fall, and do a split showing all my lady business, making a PG-13 graduation X- Rated?" She took a few deep breaths, counting in her head, remembering *Philippians 4:13* from Grandma Rose's Sunday school teachings. *"I can do all things through Christ who strengthens me."* Grandma Rose was Agni's mother; a strong black woman birthed in the backwoods of the Carolina's. She never knew her biological father but was well aware of the true Father, Son, and Holy Ghost. Grandma Rose was spiritually sculpted and believed in always putting God first with family following closely behind. Every Sunday after church she would bring the family together serving up a dose of love, faith, and soul food. Grandma Rose was very influential to her favorite grandchild who was growing impatient and delusional during the ceremony.

Then it happened. The junior marshall signaled for her row to stand to their feet. She stood in line with her head held high, rocking a fresh blowout adorned with her cap, the dignified gown covering her form fitting sunflower dress underneath, a classy French manicure, and a pair of dainty black sandals. Her short thick legs and junk in the trunk had her looking like the epitome of a true southern bell. Finally, it was time for her to walk across the stage to be awarded her hard-earned Master's Degree in Biology. She knew that the late Reverend Singleton was her guardian angel and that everything was going to be all right. She stood at the end of the stage and the announcer stated her name, "Ava Elise Singleton." Ava gracefully floated across the stage without incident, a Colgate smile adorning her face.

Ava was always told by Agni, "The only thing that can't be taken away from you in this world is your education." Ava was now deemed a triple threat in America, as she was a black educated female. Statistically speaking, she should have had a baby out of wedlock before turning eighteen, suffered from substance abuse, or been involved in criminal activity, due to being raised in a household plagued by domestic violence. Surprised by her own survival, Ava reflected on the fact the past made her physically and mentally stronger. Ava had succeeded against all odds and a new chapter was opening in her life.

CHAPTER 1

THE STRUGGLE IS REAL

Now a recent graduate, the time had come for Ava to get a real "J-O-B" like the old folks say.

"Where the hell you going? Are you trying to work at the library or LabCore Inc.?" Agni questioned Ava who was trying on potential interview outfits from her closet.

At a loss for words, Ava continued to button up her floral cardigan that she had paired with a ruffled white blouse and black dress pants. Poor thing hadn't quite grasped the complete concept of business casual and the need for an interview suit. However, Agni was on a mission to make sure her daughter was dressed for success.

Ava was accustomed to shopping on a budget at Bargain Buyz, a store that sold flawed name brand merchandise. The merchandise had failed inspections and could not be sold at the big-name department stores. It was never out of the ordinary to see a small hole in a garment from Ava's favorite store. Unashamed, she would conceal the imperfections in her garments if the price was right. Ava could hang with the best of them on the fashion scene, albeit her frugalness.

Keeping in mind the age-old motto, "Dress for the position you want, not for the position you have." Agni took Ava to the premier women's fashion store at the local mall. She had her try on a gray two-piece pencil skirt and blazer paired with a purple blouse. When Ava put on the suit, she felt like a million bucks. A strong ambient glow surrounded her as she stepped out of the fitting room.

"The gray and purple are power colors that accent the strong Beautiful Black Queen you have become."

"Thank you, Mama. How much is the suit?"

"Don't worry about the price. Everybody needs to have an investment suit in the closet."

Ava smiled until she saw the price tag of $600.00 dangling from the sleeve. Her heart dropped; $600.00 for a suit was out of the question for someone unemployed, and as for her mama, she could barely remember to pay the bills on time. Nonetheless, this didn't stop Agni from walking to the register and charging the suit to her credit card that was almost at its limit. Ava promised herself that once she got a job she would pay her mama back with interest.

Agni had to also provide for her younger children, JaQuan and Keisha who were still in high school. Unlike their older sister, they shared deadbeat Braxton as a part-time father. Now don't get it twisted, JaQuan of course is a name that is a dead giveaway on a resume, leaving no element of surprise to his race. Sure, corporate

America would see the name JaQuan and know without a doubt he was BLACK. However, despite the name, JaQuan was a yellow bone, non-name brand caring, highly intelligent, borderline genius who was finishing his senior year. His pastimes consisted of after school chess club meetings, debate team competitions, and football practices. Taking much pride in being the team's lead benchwarmer, JaQuan found solace hanging out with the football team and cheering from the sidelines.

Keisha on the other hand was the problematic child. On a good day, she embodied the behavior of Junior Healy; on a bad day, she could be Chucky reincarnated. A week without a detention slip or school suspension was a success for her. She enjoyed gossiping, writing in her diary, and twerking like typical teenage girls her age. Trying to converse with Keisha was impossible at times; you might as well be talking to a brick wall. Keisha would often disrespect her mother, most definitely a learned behavior from her sorry ass father. In Keisha's case what they say is true, when you hate someone so much you subconsciously become everything you hate. Grandma Rose always told Keisha to read *Ephesians 4:31-32. "Let all bitterness, and wrath, and anger, and clamor, and evil speaking, be put away from you, with all malice. And be kind to one another, tenderhearted, forgiving one another, even as God in Christ's forgave you."* For all that was wrong with Keisha, an outsider looking in would never know she was damaged. Keisha had beautiful brown skin, long natural hair, and a full figure. She was simply trying to take on the world in her own way.

The morning of the job interview Ava got dressed in her "new

3

investment suit." She went into the interview room dressed to impress, embodying the confidence of a politician. Surprisingly, Ava knew she had out dressed the interviewer stepping into the room. The interviewer had her nose so far up in the air she had to be Uncle Tom's kinfolk. Her aura screamed of arrogance and new money. This black woman had just been promoted and was feeling herself more than a 2-ply roll of Soft Touch toilet tissue. Unfortunately, she had no interest in molding another young black woman to be successful and was only concerned with self. You know, the typical "crabs in a barrel" syndrome.

"What can you tell me about yourself?" The boredom was already apparent as the interviewer played with her fingernails. Clearing her throat, Ava demanded her attention.

"Well, I recently graduated with my Master's Degree in Biology, and I'm ready to further cultivate my skills. My classroom studies have given me the knowledge to perform proficiently at LabCore Inc. making me an invaluable asset to your team."

"Okay, what can you tell me about LabCore Inc.?" She nonchalantly echoed, just like her off-putting mom jeans and paper thin polyester blouse.

Unfazed by the egotism of the interviewer, Ava had done her homework and shot off a well-informed answer ever-so eloquently.

"LabCore Inc. provides innovative testing in special and clinical laboratories throughout the world. Hundreds of thousands of specimens are tested daily, doubling the production of most other private competitors. The company continues to make significant advances that are constantly recognized by the scientific community."

"How do you see yourself benefiting LabCore Inc. in five years?" She asked, staring with piercing big bug eyes.

"In five years, I would like to have already advanced from an entry level position to a Quality Team Leader. I will successfully take on and complete additional responsibilities with any position I hold. I would also like to help with new research studies anytime the opportunity presents itself."

She nodded, still seething with jealousy directed toward the educated and qualified black woman sitting in front of her. After a moment, she thanked Ava for her time. Ava left the interviewer and the room with her head held high. A week later LabCore Inc. informed Ava that she did not receive the position. The news was delivered riddled with the underlying premise of being "overqualified."

The setback was slightly discouraging. However, within a few days Ava was hired to work at the local Ale Right Brewing Company through a temporary agency. She was making $15.00 an hour as an entry level microbiologist. Unhappy, she sat around cooped up in a laboratory. The pressure of maintaining good manufacturing practices and monitoring the microbe growth in the beer was tedious for Ava. It also didn't help that the economy was on a downward spiral, and major corporations were finding shortcuts to save money. By hiring temporary employees through staffing agencies, corporate America learned they didn't have to pay insurance or provide health benefits to their workers. Upwards of 80% of recent graduates were returning home from college to live with their parents.

Ava knew that she was blessed to have a job, but $15.00 an hour wasn't great taking into consideration the sky-rocketing price of gas, health expenses without insurance, and lack of necessary 401K investments. Consequently, social security benefits were soon to be non-existent for Americans. Ava knew that she needed to make more money, as her monthly birth control pills alone costed $75.00 without insurance. She would have to stay focused applying for other jobs because this could not be her future; rather another setback for a stronger comeback.

One hot humid afternoon Ava was driving home from Ale Right Brewing Company. She was jamming to the Hot 106.2 Hip-Hop Station when a commercial caught her attention. The broadcast was recruiting new police officers to join the Minor Hills Police Department's 34th Police Basic Introductory Class. They were looking for brave men and women to protect and serve the community. The Minor Hills Police Department had a paid academy class that included health benefits and provided a supplemental bonus for having a college education. Ava thought this could be a stepping stone into a career as a crime scene investigator or a platform for the federal government. The benefits sounded appeasing and she didn't want to miss any opportunities. Ava decided that she didn't have anything to lose and gave the recruiter a ring.

Ava sat in her bedroom with the door closed speaking to the recruiter, well versed in the potential for Keisha and JaQuan to talk loudly. She spoke with excessive pride, detailing her recent accomplishment of obtaining her Master's degree, and her eagerness to serve the community. Impressed, the recruiter provided further insight into the police world, explaining that police work is about honor, courage, bravery, and the ability to serve the public. The recruiter insisted Ava apply ASAP in an effort to meet the rapidly approaching deadline. It was also recommended that she complete a ride along with an Officer Pendleton to see firsthand what an officer does on a daily basis.

Confined to her bedroom, Ava completed all the prescreening questionnaires and release forms for the application. She quickly realized the hiring process was not a joke and that she would have to complete each of the following: Comprehensive Exam, Psychological Test, Physical Fitness Ability Test, Drug Test, Polygraph Test, Medical Test, and Oral Board Review. The requirements were strenuous to say the least, the Mt. Everest of hiring processes. She thought that this would be a great opportunity to serve her community. While also affording her the ability to help Agni in raising JaQuan and Keisha. This could be her "big break", opening the door to a broad spectrum of future career opportunities. The fact of the matter was Ava couldn't leave town in good conscience, not until she ensured JaQuan and Keisha ended up in college and not the streets. Deadbeat Braxton didn't care about their futures, so Ava felt compelled to put the burden on her shoulders. With earnest efforts, she decided to complete the hiring process whole heartedly. Standing by faith, Ava knew the job was already hers.

"Hello, I just submitted my application online. I also set up an appointment with Officer Pendleton to do a ride along. Thank you again for the opportunity and I look forward to hearing from you soon." Relieved, the voicemail left on the recruiter's phone sounded enthusiastic just as she had practiced.

Two weeks later, Ava reported to the 2nd Police Plaza at 1100 hours for her first ride along. An old Crown Victoria pulled up in front of Ava and the driver's window slowly rolled down. A black woman with smooth dark skin and strong facial features, characteristic of her African ancestors, was sitting in the driver's seat. Ava observed a little "pimp" in her walk as she exited the patrol vehicle. It was safe to assume that she lived an alternative lifestyle. She was approximately 6'0 ft. tall, skinny build, and approximately one hundred and fifty pounds. Seeing the officer reminded Ava of an incident back in high school, when a "butch" teammate tried to rub her inner thighs. As a few expletives rolled off her tongue, Ava swatted her arm away to clarify such advances were not welcomed. She wasn't homophobic and loved people for people, but cupcake smashing wasn't Ava's thing.

The lady introduced herself as Officer Pendleton. Ava was ecstatic to be doing her ride along with a black woman. Especially one that could successfully get away with rocking a bald head. Touching her own head, Ava didn't think she could pull it off and jumped in the passenger seat.

Driving around town the two engaged in small talk. Both women were college educated, athletic, easy going, and passionate about helping the Minor Hills community. While they were chatting, Ava learned that Pendleton had lost her father to heart disease. At this moment, something hit Ava and she realized why she was truly interested in a career in law enforcement. Being raised in a household that resembled a constant warzone, Ava fought whenever Braxton put his hands on her mother. Though she never actually won the physical fights, Ava's will to fight remained intact. She would never back down from anyone who disrespected her mother, no matter the consequences. Ava wanted to take that same fight inside of her to benefit the community. *Luke 10:3, "Go your way: behold, I send you as lambs among wolves."*

Ava was beginning to "get in her feelings," as Pendleton keyed up on the radio, "Car 1-2-2, I'll be 10-38."

The dispatcher acknowledged simultaneously with Ava snapping out of her emotional moment of self-reflection. The next thing Ava knew, Pendleton was stopping a red Cavalier at the intersection of Martin Luther King Jr. Dr. at Peachtree St.

Promptly, Pendleton told communications, "Alpha-Tom-Charlie-X-X-X-X." Ava's hesitation was readily apparent as her seatbelt was still securely fastened.

"Take my flashlight and stand behind me. If you see any contraband let me know. Oh! If shit hits the fan, here is the shotgun release button." Pendleton pointed to a black button near the ignition.

Ava 's heart dropped, "Yeah, so I've never used a shotgun before, Officer Pendleton."

"Above the trigger is the safety button. Once you push the safety, the shotgun is in a ready position. Just point at the target and squeeze the trigger."

"I believe I can handle that." Ava replied slightly content after the quick crash course of Shooting 101. Secretly, Ava prayed that she wouldn't have to pump holes into anyone's body.

Pendleton made a driver's side approach with Ava closely behind. The driver rolled down the window.

"Can I have your driver's license and registration please, sir?" Pendleton asked.

"Yes sir." The driver had mistaken Pendleton for a man.

"My system shows you have an expired registration and a suspended driver's license. I'm a woman by the way."

"I'm so sorry ma'am it's been a long day. I have been trying to get myself together financially, so I can pay off some tickets."

Ava didn't observe any contraband and giggled on the inside, because Pendleton had assertively and professionally put the driver in his place. Once the driver handed over the requested information the ladies returned to the car.

"What should I do, Future Officer Singleton?" Hastily, throwing the ball in Ava's court.

Pondering, "Everyone deserves a break every now and again."

"I'd give him a warning ticket."

Ava reflected on her numerous speeding tickets, wishing someone would have cut her a break. Another police officer stopped by while Pendleton was typing out the warning ticket. It turns out, they were in a high crime area where officers are obliged to routinely check on each other. Ava was impressed with the unforgettable camaraderie. The driver was informed that he should thank Future Officer Singleton for cutting him a break and wait for a licensed driver to move his vehicle. Ava knew that as soon as they got around the corner the driver was going to be driving again. On the other hand, she didn't particularly want to spend her entire ride along on a traffic stop babysitting. Ava loved how Pendleton handled her business. The way she did it was quite genius. She couldn't assume any liability if the driver made the decision to unlawfully operate the vehicle because the warning ticket had been documented electronically. Also, by not babysitting the man, Pendleton was showing that she trusted the driver to make the best decision. Without hesitation emergency tones could be heard from Pendleton's car radio.

"Car 1-2-2."

"Go ahead," Pendleton responded.

"I need you to respond to 1st and Mack St. in reference to an unknown problem, man down."

"En-route," she replied with urgency.

"Should be a black male wearing a Carolina blue jacket and gray sweatpants laying down at the bus stop. Unknown if patient is breathing normally. Caller is a passerby."

Pendleton activated her emergency lights and sirens, putting the Crown Victoria into high gear. Ava sat in the passenger seat holding on for dear life. Crazy thoughts were running through Ava's head: What if the man wrote a check his ass couldn't cash? Is it just a homeless guy who started drinking his forty a little too early? Or even worse, what if this guy is dead? Before Ava could finish her thoughts, Pendleton slammed on the brakes.

"We are here." She jumped out of the car with Ava trailing skittishly behind. A black male laid on the bus stop bench matching the description. The man had at least six open containers of malt liquor surrounding him. Ava could tell the man was breathing due to his obnoxious snoring. Instantly relieved, she realized they hadn't rolled up on a dead body.

"Detail, wake up," stated Pendleton.

"Detail" was nothing more than the neighborhood alcoholic who washed cars to support his addiction. He got around town on his bicycle, equipped with two beat up wash buckets hanging from the handlebars. More often than not, members of the community would actually pay Detail to stay away from their cars. Ava could only wonder what life event lead him to living on the streets.

Officer Pendleton became more assertive and yelled louder, "Detail, wake up!"

A disoriented Detail had finally awakened. He was dark skinned, short-statured, with a non-athletic build. To Ava it appeared Detail was on a downward spiral resulting from bad life decisions. He tried to maintain his balance as he slowly came to his feet, bracing himself against the bench. Detail began to walk away. However, he lost his footing and nearly landed in the middle of the street.

Pendleton had reached her breaking point, "I'm taking you to jail under a 24-Hour Intoxicated Subject Hold. You are currently a danger to yourself and others."

"Well let's go honey. It's Fried Fish Friday at the jail and a brother not trying to miss lunch." Detail stated carelessly placing his hands behind his back, trying to expedite the process.

Ava was flooded with mixed emotions; she wanted to laugh hysterically although she was deeply disturbed. Never in her life had she witnessed a grown man rushing to get a free meal at the county jail, compliments of taxpaying citizens. There was no way in hell, the fried fish at the jail could stand up against any of Grandma Rose's fish fry's.

Once they arrived at the jail, Pendleton placed Detail in a small holding cell surrounded by three cement walls and steel bars. The jail cell was approximately seven feet by seven feet. A foul odor permeated through the place, comparable to a high school football team's locker room mixed with the scent of a hot boiling crockpot full of chitterlings. Ava held her breath unaccustomed to this new putrid scent. Pendleton completed the necessary paperwork and telephoned the jailers.

Moments later a sexy intake officer appeared. He was light skinned, 6'2, muscular build, and through his dress pants you could tell he wasn't lacking in the meat department. Ava forgot about holding her breath, batted her eyes, and smiled hard at the intake officer.

"Damn, who is this beauty?" The intake officer asked Pendleton.

"Future Officer Singleton. Why are you worried about it? Detail needs to be taken back because he is not trying to miss Fried Fish Friday, player."

The intake officer chuckled and when Pendleton turned her back, he quickly scribbled a note and slipped it to Ava. The note read, "Hey Beautiful, this coupon is valid for a dinner date. Call me when you get a chance. I get off work at 2100 hours, but I can be available for you 24/7."

Ava was overly flattered. A reformed player herself, she recognized the game the intake officer was playing. Now, a free meal was usually right down her alleyway, but there was no need for dinner. "Mr. Officer" was packing about twelve inches of everything she needed.

While exiting the jail, Ava realized she had worked up her own appetite, credited to Detail's excitement for Fried Fish Friday. Pendleton took Ava to Beef World, an old mom and pop shop that didn't hesitate to put more than the recommended serving size on a plate. Even better, they were "police friendly" and gave Pendleton and Ava half off their meals, alongside a free glass of southern-style sweet tea.

In the middle of eating the delicious burgers and crinkled cut fries, Pendleton began to tell Ava that police work is not for the weak. The key to not passing judgment is simply staying grounded in one's faith. *Luke 6:37 "Judge not, and ye will not be judged; condemn not, and ye shall not be condemned; forgive, and ye shall be forgiven."*

"There is something special about you Singleton. I believe wholeheartedly that you will be a great asset to this police department. Minor Hills needs to see a higher number of women making a difference in the community. Here is my number in case you have any questions."

"Officer Pendleton, thank you for showing me a glimpse into a career as a law enforcement officer. I greatly appreciate your service to our community."

CHAPTER 2

CONDITIONAL OFFER PLEASE

A few weeks later, the recruiter called Ava and scheduled her test date for that Monday at 0730 hours. Ava would have to successfully complete comprehensive, psychological, and physical examinations. The notion of completing the Police Officer's Physical Ability Test (POPAT) intimidated Ava. The POPAT consisted of exiting a patrol vehicle, running 250 yards, dragging a 175-pound dummy 75-feet, running stairs, breaching a 100-pound door, and doing 25 push-ups. If that wasn't enough, Ava would have to run another series of stairs, crawl through a 50-foot tunnel, complete 25 additional push-ups, and run 250 yards in 12 minutes and 25 seconds.

She was no stranger to working out, but physical activity had been put on the back burner while obtaining a higher education. In high school, the All Conference Female Athlete of the Year, was none other than Ava Singleton. Ava was a great contribution to the women's varsity tennis, soccer, basketball, and track teams.

Ava had been promoted to tennis Captain when she was only a sophomore, leading her doubles partner to the Regional Conference. On the soccer field, she was given the nickname "Peanut." The competitors often underestimated Ava's strength due to her small stature. Quite a few females learned the hard way, after being taken down by Ava's signature slide tackle. Ava's speed came in handy playing fullback, stopping the opponent's fast running forwards. She was also the prettiest point guard whose crossover was reminiscent of Allen Iverson in his prime. The boys varsity basketball team would always watch Ava play before their games. They admired Ava's body and "beast-mode" on the court.

Even the track coach asked Ava to help the team in running the 800-meter relay at District Conference, after witnessing her running in top speed. Unfortunately, Ava didn't realize she would have to run two laps around the track and over-exerted herself. She took off too fast, caught a cramp, and ended up walking the second lap. People in the stands cheered Ava on, hoping to get her off the track swiftly. Spectators were ready to proceed with the next event that was being delayed by Ava. Understandably, Ava's days on the track team were short lived and slightly embarrassing. However, sports offered Ava a temporary oasis from being in a household beset with domestic violence. More importantly, sports taught Ava many life lessons including discipline, hard-work, and sportsmanship. Ava translated the lessons to values she carried over in everyday life.

Ava began strenuous training for the POPAT, knowing prior

preparation would prevent poor performance. The first step for Ava was downloading the application "Lazy Ass to 5K" on her smart phone. Monday through Friday she pushed herself to new fitness extremes, becoming more confident in her physical abilities. Ava would do practice POPAT tests using Agni's lovely staircase for the steps, Keisha as the one hundred and seventy-five-pound dummy that would have to be dragged, and the neighborhood streets to run like Rocky Balboa. The practice never stopped as Ava was subconsciously a perfectionist. Plus, she wasn't worried about the psychological or written examination. In her mind, she couldn't be crazier than the other Carolina bumpkins walking around.

Rising early, Ava reported to the Minor Hills Public Training Center with thirty minutes to spare. She couldn't risk being on colored people time, as that would be truly unacceptable in the law enforcement profession. Ava was sent to a classroom with fifty-five other candidates.

An officer came into the classroom and stated, "In a few minutes you will be taking the comprehensive examination. It will measure basic reading, mathematics, comprehension, and analytical reasoning. You will have one hour to complete the test. After you complete the test, I will grade it immediately. If you score below a 70 you will be asked to leave and may reapply to the Minor Hill's Police Department after a year's time. Are there any questions?"

Ava sat in the room amongst her peers and realized that she was the only black female present. Demographically, the candidates consisted of thirty-eight white males, four black males, a Hispanic male, and twelve white females. She thought to herself, if I can pass this test the job should be mine. Ava was well-built, standing without the assistance of affirmative action and equal opportunity-based employment. The officer began to pass out test booklets. Anxious, Ava prayed a small prayer, "Dear Heavenly Father, I come before you humble and with a grateful heart. I know that faith without substance is not evident. I know that these test questions are only a formality and that I have already passed. I claim it in your name, Jesus. Thank you. Amen."

Ava opened the test booklet and saw what appeared to be an end of grade test for a fifth grader.

"Yes! Thank you, Jesus! I can handle this!" Ava silently rejoiced knowing her prayers had been answered.

The first five questions were based off a George Washington Carver passage. Ava didn't have to read the passage to answer the questions. This was the same young lady who had her Master's Degree in Biology. She had researched and respected the former slave who became one of the greatest scientists of the 20th century. George Washington Carver invented over three hundred products from simply using peanuts. Not to mention, George Washington Carver had been acknowledged for rescuing the agricultural economy of the rural south.

A part of Ava was almost insulted they had her answering simplistic questions based on American history. She was thankful that her mother Agni had her reading books about black history at an early age. Ava completed the rest of the test with ease and was the first candidate to submit her exam. She looked around and saw the other candidates with their heads buried in the test booklet. Surely, they weren't struggling she rationalized to herself. The officer took the test answer sheet and placed it through a Scantron machine.

"Congratulations you passed. Go take a break. The Psychological Test will begin shortly."

"Thank you." Ava was excited but displayed a calm demeanor. Ava was sitting in the lobby for only a short while, before being summoned back to the classroom for the Psychological Test. The officer resumed, "Unfortunately some of your peers did not pass the comprehensive examination. We will be taking the Psychological Test next. If you fail this test, again you will be asked to leave and should wait a year to reapply. If you pass this test, you will have the opportunity to complete the POPAT. Once you complete these tests successfully, you will advance in the hiring process. Do you have any questions?"

No one in the classroom raised their hand. Ava looked around and realized there was only one black male left in the classroom. The other minorities had failed the comprehensive examination. Ava wondered if the George Washington Carver passage was a challenge for them. She silently wished the black community would reinforce the value of education over wearing the latest kicks. She knew firsthand black families that would make sure they had the latest pair of "J's" before concerning themselves with a rent payment. Even worse, some blacks would kill to have the expensive shoes on their feet. Now we all know Ava had a couple of "J's" in the closet growing up too. However, if her grades weren't up to par, Agni would have her rocking the "We Not Reebok Classics" to class, without a second thought.

Abruptly, the officer began passing out the tests. Staring at the test with five hundred questions, Ava's head began to throb. If Ava wasn't crazy already, she would be after answering all those questions. Ava attempted to answer the questions in order, but came to a standstill, after noticing she was skipping the same question, asked in different ways: *Have you ever stolen something? Have you ever taken something that did not belong to you and failed to return it? Are you a kleptomaniac?* Ava wondered if lying about how many doughnuts being in a bag or sampling the grapes at the grocery store was technically considered stealing? Well since she had paid for a few of the doughnuts and the grapes were just samples, Ava reasoned a solid "no" to all those questions would suffice. She completed the rest of the questions knowing that it was all in God's hands. Ava took her test to the officer to be graded.

"You passed! Go get dressed in your athletic wear and return to the lobby for further instructions." The officer advised Ava who was happier than a fat kid at the dessert portion of the buffet line.

In preparation for the POPAT Test, Ava began chanting lyrics to her favorite hype song by Archie Eversole featuring Bubba Sparxxx. "We Ready! We Ready! We Ready! For Ya'll! Come on!"

Ava sat in the lobby patiently, realizing only twenty candidates remained. She and the lone black male were the only minorities to advance forward through the testing phase. By growing up in a black community briefly, Ava understood that there was mistrust with the police. In the 1970s, America was known for multiple incidents involving police brutality against African Americans. Older African Americans believed that most police officers were members of the Ku Klux Klan, using their authority to discriminate against the black community. These reasons alone likely played a role in why only 12% of minorities applied for the job with the Minor Hills Police Department.

The officer came into the lobby and directed the candidates outside to begin the POPAT test. A physical fitness instructor demonstrated the test and asked for a volunteer to go first. After sizing up the competition, Ava raised her hand and jumped in the patrol vehicle. She unfastened her seatbelt, exited the patrol vehicle, and ran out of the driver's side door. The 175-pound dummy was heavier than anticipated. Thinking fast, she grabbed the legs of the dummy and threw it around her neck slowly back-pedaling. Along the way, Ava stepped on a hard rock, causing a mild sprain in her left ankle. Ava knew that she had to keep pushing. During the series of steps, she hopped her way up and down. She placed most of the pressure on her right foot to alleviate the pain.

Ava caught her breath while staring at the 100-pound door that she needed to breach. With both hands on the door, she pushed without the door bulging. Quickly assessing the situation, Ava lowered her body weight by squatting, and pushed into the door using her shoulders. The door opened slowly and Ava shimmied her way through. She completed the push-ups and sit ups with ease, relieved to be off her feet. The tunnel was pitch dark so she closed her eyes and crawled through. Hell, not being able to see was nothing new, Ava was farsighted and couldn't see up close on a good day. The end of the course was near, 25 push-ups and sit ups down. Digging deep, she sprinted the last 250 yards. Ava completed the test with five minutes to spare.

"Wonderful job, Ms. Singleton. You are scheduled to complete a Drug Test and Medical Assessment next Wednesday at 1400 hours. Does that work for you?" The officer stated while holding a clipboard.

"Yes. Thank you again." Ava replied refreshed with a new surge of energy.

On Wednesday Ava went to the Medical Services Center. She was requested to remove all items from her pockets, hover over a toilet, urinate in a specimen cup, and to not flush. Ava knew she had never smoked a joint in her life. However, she couldn't account for the many contact highs and long party nights during her undergraduate career. Next, Ava completed a hearing test.

"Dang girl, if you would have missed another beep you would have been out of the door." The nurse stated.

Ava just smiled at the nurse. She was a child of God, blessed and highly favored. It would take more than a few beeps to keep Ava away from seeking permanent employment.

The recruiter called and informed Ava that she would have to successfully complete a Polygraph Test and Oral Board Review before receiving a conditional offer. Ava understood that the test symbolized minor obstacles along her continued journey to self-betterment. Replaying past episodes of *Jerry Springer* and *The Maury Show*, Ava recounted the damage caused by the lie detector tests. Nervous, Ava began researching how to beat polygraph tests in multiple search engines online. She learned that the polygraph machine looks for inconsistencies in physiological characteristics, such as pulse rates and breathing patterns. Ava knew that she would have to remain calm, focusing on her breathing and heart rate. She figured they would ask her the basic questions. Have you ever smoked weed? Have you ever sold drugs? Have you lied thus far in the application process?

In high school, she drove a "dope boy" down the street on a lunch break to sell a dime bag of weed. Ava only did that to make a little extra gas money. At the time, her mother Agni was going through a gruesome divorce with "fuckboy" Braxton. Trying to get back on her feet Agni had to live below her means, raising three children in an extended stay hotel. Ava quickly withdrew the "dope boy transport" from her memory bank because the Polygraph Test would soon arrive.

Before she knew it, the secretary told Ava to have a seat as the examiner would be with her shortly. The examiner was an older white male, gray-haired, blue-eyed, with a few extra pounds hanging over his belt. He escorted Ava to the examination room.

"Hey, I'm going to hook up a few wires to you. Stay still and focus on the square in front of you." The examiner requested in a serious tone.

"Yes sir." Ava replied, focusing on her breathing while controlling her heart rate without being completely obvious.

"Now I'm going to ask you a series of base questions. Is your name Ava Singleton?"

"Yes sir." She responded balling up her feet inside of her shoes to conceal the nervousness. All the wires on Ava's body had her feeling like a scientific experiment.

"Are you twenty-three years old?"

"Yes sir."

"We will begin the test now. Have you been honest throughout the hiring process?"

"Yes sir."

"Have you ever made any threatening phone calls?"

"Yes sir, during my sorority days as an undergraduate. Nothing too bad though."

"Have you had any additional traffic violations besides the three speeding tickets you show on your record?"

"No sir. Not that I'm aware of."

"Do you have any ulterior motives for joining the Minor Hills Police Department."

"No sir."

"Have you participated in any major crimes?

"No sir."

"Have you been involved in any crimes against nature?"

"No sir." Ava replied with disgust.

"Have you ever stolen anything?"

After taking a deep breath she replied slowly, "Yes sir. I had a bad habit of walking to the store to get donuts. I would lie to the store clerk about how many donuts were actually in my bag."

"That completes the test. I will return shortly with your results." The examiner chuckled struggling to maintain his composure.

Ava sat slightly doubtful in the room, hoping she hadn't said too much. The overwhelming pressure forced a confession from the reformed donut thief. She tried to stay calm knowing there had to be a camera recording her every move.

Returning to the room the examiner stated, "Ms. Singleton, you passed the test. However, you did show deception when you were asked, "Have you participated in any major crimes?""

"Sir. I have not participated in any major crimes." Ava replied, in a shocked soft voice.

"I was just joking with you."

Ava put on her professional laugh as the examiner directed her back to the lobby.

"An officer will be down briefly so you can complete the final phase of the hiring process, the Oral Board Review."

Ava sat in the lobby praying she would remember to use the "Queen's English" and not any words from Grandma Rose's dialect. Grandma Rose could not always enunciate her words properly. For example, any word that began with an S-T-R was treacherous territory for her. The word "strawberry" would be pronounced "Shaw-Barry" and the word "street" would be pronounced "Sh-eet."

A well-dressed police officer with a crisp uniform entered the lobby. He was a middle-aged white man with a steroid induced muscular build, dark brown hair, and green eyes. He introduced himself as Lieutenant Livingstone.

"Right this way, Ms. Singleton. We have been waiting to meet you."

Ava followed Lt. Livingstone into a conference room where a panel of eight male officers were seated. Words couldn't describe how uncomfortable Ava felt, being the only female and minority in the room. It brought back memories of being a young child walking to the store. A group of white men had pulled up beside Ava in a truck hollering, "I hate Niggers! Niggers! Niggers! Stunned, she stood fixated on the 6-foot noose dragging from the back of the truck with a confederate flag plastered in the back window. Ava could only suspect they were a part of the Ku Klux Klan.

Ava was the only black person outside and knew the derogatory comments were directed at her. Hitting Olympic speeds she ran home to tell her mother. Once Agni heard the news, she grabbed a wooden baseball bat and drove to the store. Thank goodness, the truck was gone because Agni would've forever been identified as Inmate 16543, to say the least. Ava stopped reminiscing and held her head up high, confidently clothed in her "investment suit." Looking at her purple blouse Ava remembered the strong and confident black woman she had become. Ava could only hope the men in uniform stood for liberty and justice for all.

Lt. Livingstone requested Ava take a seat. Ava sat down just like she had practiced with Agni; ankles crossed, knees together, back straight, and a modest smile for the panel.

"Can you tell me a little bit about yourself?" Lt. Livingstone asked.

"Yes sir, my name is Ava Singleton and it is very nice to meet you all. I recently obtained my Master's degree from Minor Hills Agricultural & Technical State University. I am a well-rounded, hardworking, self-motivated, multi-faceted team player looking for a career change." She made eye contact with the entire panel while speaking.

"What made you apply for this job when your background is in Biology?" Lt. Livingstone began prying into Ava, seeming puzzled as he read over her resume.

"To be honest…I imagine myself being a hardcore detective like Olivia Benson from *Law & Order: Special Victims Unit*. More importantly it will provide me the opportunity to protect and serve the Minor Hills community."

"Why are you leaving your current job?"

"I have learned a lot working in the microbiology department at Ale Right Brewing Company, but I'm ready for a new challenge. I would like to increase my analytical reasoning skills. I believe this could be achieved working at the Minor Hill's Police Department."

"What is your weakness? The recruiter has already called and asked your mother the answer to this question." He questioned, slightly raising one eyebrow in an intimidating manner.

"I have a "Type A Personality" and I like to complete one task expeditiously before starting another. However, I have learned in the workforce that you must complete and work on several tasks at a time. I have attended workshops that have improved my organizational and time management skills. Now, I can successfully complete multiple tasks at a time."

"How would your friends describe you?" A younger officer asked in a warmhearted tone.

"My friends will tell you that I'm well-spoken, goal-oriented, and passionate. In college, I served as the Vice President of my sorority where I had to plan, coordinate, organize, and delegate tasks. While holding my position, I had the opportunity to implement new fundraisers which provided multiple scholarships to high school graduates." The barrage of questions seemed to last an eternity, but Ava remained focused.

Lt. Livingstone questioned the panel, "Do you guys have any more questions for Ms. Singleton?" The panel of officers shook their heads "no," appearing sufficiently satisfied with the interview.

"Well, Ms. Singleton, do you have any questions for us?" Lt. Livingstone asked wrapping things up.

"Yes sir. How long is the Police Academy?"

"The Police Academy is a rigorous six-month program. Once you have successfully completed the program you will complete three months of Field Training before being released for solo assignment." Lt. Livingstone was very forthright.

"Thank you, sir."

"Do you have any further questions?"

"No sir. Thank you all for your time and this opportunity."

Ava's hands were sweating profusely from being in the hot seat. She discreetly dried her hands off in the seat where her thighs rested. The combination of fortitude and sass built into her was apparent as Ava gave each member of the interview panel a firm handshake. Lt. Livingstone escorted her back to the lobby and thanked her for being a breath of fresh air.

"Expect to hear back from us before the week is out so we can schedule an appointment to discuss your conditional offer."

"Thank you, sir, I look forward to hearing from you all soon." Ava's right palm started itching instantly. The old folks insisted that was a sign money was on the way.

Two days later the recruiter called, "Ms. Singleton, congratulations you have been granted a conditional offer. I need you to come by the Human Resource Department at the Police Plaza to review the offer."

"Thank you, Jesus!" Ava broke out in a victory dance.

She gratefully accepted the conditional offer and the $10,000.00 educational bonus.

CHAPTER 3

RECRUITS ON YOUR FEET!!

The first of September, Ava reported to the Minor Hills Public Safety Training Center at 0700 hours. She entered a smart classroom equipped with a computer, projector, DVD player, interactive white board, and forty-two recruits. A few recruits were placing their books on the desks, others were chatting away about the hiring process, and the rest looked a bit nervous as if World War III was steadily approaching. Recruits were assigned seats based on the alphabetical order of their last name. The class was comprised of fourteen females and twenty-eight males. This class had the largest number of female recruits in Minor Hills' history. The female recruits consisted of ten whites, three blacks, and one Latina; the male recruits included twenty-three whites, four blacks, and one Latino.

Ava overheard one of the female recruits saying, "Girl, this is my third time applying to the Minor Hills Police Department. I finally got it this time though."

The recruits looked like a bunch of mall cops because they were forced to wear a hideous gray collared shirt with a black tie, creased pants, and boots. Around their waist was a duty belt that contained a fictitious red handgun, taser carrier, empty magazine holder, inert mace, radio, and handcuffs.

Moments later Sergeant Evans marched into the center of the floor and began yelling, "Recruits on your feet now! I don't remember getting the memo that we were hiring members of the geriatric population! What is taking so long for you all to get on your feet?"

Sgt. Evans was approximately 55 years of age, 6'5, gray hair, piercing blue eyes, muscular build, and appeared to be prior military due to his demeanor. The recruits stood with their feet together and hands behind their back in a parade rest position. Ava's heart pounded, flabbergasted by the quick change of pace.

"Behind me you will see a shadow box with forty-two badges. You will earn your badge. If you do not have the heart for this job you will ring the bell beside the shadow box. Minor Hills Police Department is not for the weak ladies and gentlemen. The badge itself is a $3.00 piece of metal that stands for much more. The badge represents honor, courage, peace, bravery, dignity, and fidelity. You should be very proud that you are standing here today. We received nine hundred and fifty-four applications and you are the forty-two that were selected. Prior military, get the recruits in formation and have them at the flag poles by 0800 hours." Sgt. Evans stated bluntly.

Recruit Ford spoke up, "Sir, yes sir." Ford had joined the army when he graduated high school and had been honorably discharged after completing a tour in Iraq.

Ford got the 34th Police Basic Introductory Class in formation. While the recruits were standing in formation facing the American flag, ten stern uniformed police officers came outside along with Sgt. Evans. "Hell Day" had officially begun. Ava reminisced about pledging the best sorority in the world. If she could deal with a large group of educated black women, she could deal with anything they threw at her.

In a strident tone, Sgt. Evans continued to bark out orders, "You will report in formation every morning at 0800 hours. We will put up the flags and conduct daily inspections."

He then began walking up and down visually inspecting each recruit from head to toe. Suddenly, he came to a hasty stop in front of Recruit Owens.

"Why in the hell is your name tag on backwards, son?"

"I'm a screw up, sir." Owens replied.

Sgt. Evans was furious, "Yes you are, and since you are, everyone else is a screw up too. Recruits drop down and do twenty-five push-ups and thank Mr. Owens."

Once the push-ups were complete Sgt. Evans continued inspecting the recruits. The other officers were standing by like hound dogs ready to pounce.

He then stopped at Recruit Huffman, "Do you suffer from halitosis son?"

"No sir," Huffman uttered out.

"Why is there fucking candy in your magazine holster? Are you going to throw breath mints if someone shoots at you? Are you going to huff and puff till someone falls down? From now on you will be referred to as Recruit Candy Man!"

"Yes sir, Recruit Candy Man I am." Huffman replied with a smirk on his face.

"Recruits hit the fire tower steps and thank Recruit Candy Man!"

Ava's ham hock legs were perfect for the staircase runs. However, she could see that it was taking a toll on some of the other recruits. She encouraged her fellow recruits to push themselves. After several rounds of going up and down the fire tower, the recruits went back inside to the classroom. Another member of the command staff introduced himself as Corporal Price.

He informed the recruits they would be taking a test every week and a score of 70 or above would be considered passing. If a test was failed, a recruit would have one additional retest. If the additional test was failed, it would be grounds for dismissal from the program. Once a recruit had failed out of the program, they would have to wait an additional year to reapply for the next police academy. Ava had her mind made up that failing was not an option and that she would have to treat police academy like a full-time J-O-B. Cpl. Price provided an outline on the various test subjects which included Constitutional Law, Standardized Field Sobriety Tests, Physical Fitness, Crime Prevention, Firearms, Civil Processes, First Responder, Arrest Techniques, and Defensive Driving. The recruits were dismissed for a thirty-minute lunch break.

De facto segregation was taking its seat in the lobby while the recruits ate. Oftentimes when people meet for the first time in institutionalized settings, they automatically feel safe when sticking to their race. Ava ate her homemade turkey and cheese sandwich while making small talk with the other black women.

"Hey ladies, I'm Ava, born and raised in Minor Hills."

"Nice to meet you. I'm Aisha from Baltimore, the Charm City."

"Call me Taylor and please excuse me for a minute. My mom is outside with my lunch plate from the Chicken Box."

"Aisha, I love your hair." Ava was impressed with the two-strand twist-out.

Giggling Aisha replied, "Girl, this isn't my real hair. It's crochet braids."

The young women laughed. Taylor returned with her chicken plate. It was apparent that she was an old soul who had a close relationship with her mother. Taylor and Ava favored, both being short-statured with matching brown skin and hair slicked back into low sitting ponytails. It would take a while for the command staff to tell them apart, since "all black people look alike" anyway.

The small talk was short lived as the recruits were summoned back to the classroom. The physical demands of the morning had pushed one of the recruits over the edge. Recruit Whitt, who was later given the nickname Recruit "Quit" was standing at the bell beside Sgt. Evans.

"Here stands Recruit Whitt who realized this job is not for him and is no longer wasting our time. Recruit Whitt do you have anything to say?"

"I'm sorry, but my heart is not in it. I wish you all the best with the Minor Hills Police Department." Whitt rang the bell and exited the classroom with tears in his eyes.

One recruit down after the first day. Sgt. Evans opened the shadow box and removed Recruit Whitt's badge. Cpl. Price entered the classroom shortly after and began teaching Ethics. The man was a self-proclaimed redneck. Ava had been raised to believe that a redneck was a white person from the country. Someone who believed the world would be better off submitting blacks to slavery and inequalities. In her mind, the typical redneck wore the confederate flag on a camouflage t-shirt, blue jeans, and cowboy boots. Growing up a few of her white friends would say, "I'm a redneck and the flag is just worn to represent our heritage."

Even so, the flag was also her heritage, but that was a fight for another day. Ava tried to remain open-minded. Ava could care less if he was a redneck, long as he provided her with the necessary information to pass the class.

The daily schedules of the recruits consisted of morning inspections, classroom lectures, thirty-minute lunch breaks, physical training, and cleaning up the facility before dismissal. Ava was adjusting to the para-military life. After a day of police academy, she would come home to review her studies. Then it would be time to eat, take a shower, and hit the bed by 2030 hours. Exhausted, Ava cancelled her cable services. After all, there weren't enough hours in the day to enjoy TV shows in addition to the demands of the academy. On top of everything, Ava didn't have much of a dating life. Occasionally, Ava found time to chat with her best guy friend from high school.

The two dated all of a week in school. It wasn't quite the puppy love type relationship either. See, Ava had been the four eyed, flat chested, nerd in middle school. In high school, the tides turned. Ava was everybody's "Woman Crush Wednesday" before the hashtag. Relationship-wise, she never could take her best guy friend seriously because he ruthlessly antagonized her back in the day. Secretly, she just dated him a week for revenge.

Blacker than night was Ava's best guy friend. Surprisingly, he loved wrestling and had big dreams of leaving the hood. Sadly, he was arrested for fitting the typical description of a robbery suspect in college. You know the "typical description" a black man, wearing a white t-shirt, shoulder length dreads, and dark blue jeans. Of course, the police determined that he wasn't the suspect. However, he fit the description, just like every other young black man living in the neighborhood.

He told Ava, "I could not do what you are doing. All my family has been to jail. Shit! A "pig" arrested me because I'm black with dreads."

"I'm sorry that you had to go through that. I'm just trying to make a difference in the community and make a better life for myself overall."

Ava understood all too well where he was coming from and

wanted to help bridge the gap between the community and law enforcement. It was important for members in lower economic communities to see minorities in law enforcement to rebuild trust.

This reminded Ava why she was standing outside in the hot beaming sun, waiting for daily inspections. Ava stood there overly confident with her new Brazilian Keratin Treatment that made her hair straighter than a ruler. Ava knew she was a "cutie from the House of Beauty." Sgt. Evans and Cpl. Price began randomly selecting recruits to visually inspect or ask 10 codes. The recruits would have to learn the proper 10 codes to effectively communicate with officers after the police academy ended.

"Recruit Owens, 10-7?" Cpl. Price asked direct.

"Out of service, sir." Owens replied desperate to redeem himself from Hell Day. Cpl. Price nodded and continued with inspections.

Without warning Cpl. Price stopped in front of Ava, "Your hair looks a hot mess! Give me twenty-five."

The old saying, "You can take a child out the ghetto, but you can't take the ghetto out the child" was in full effect. Ava stood with a flushed red face and her fists clinched.

Recruit Jones was standing to the left of Ava and Recruit Bell stood to her right. Jones was struggling to maintain his composure, presuming Ava was going to flip her switch. He was a black male, twenty-four years of age, with an athletic build. Bell was a naive twenty-year old white female, who had no idea what happens when you disrespect a black woman and her hair.

Growing up, Ava would sit down on the floor, while her mother detangled her curly kinks with a wide tooth comb. The comb would slide down the root of Ava's hair and hit a knot every now and again. Ava's head would be subjected to tension coming from her scalp. Ava was aware that if she complained, Agni would hit her in the back of the head with the comb out of frustration. The combing would continue as Agni had to comb pass the knot. Then if that wasn't enough, Ava's hair would be washed, conditioned, dried, and styled. This trauma alone likely played a pivotal role in Ava developing into a strong black woman. Ava looked at Cpl. Price and lost all self-control as she recalled him being a self-proclaimed redneck.

"Move out my damn way! Your push-ups don't faze me!" She pushed Cpl. Price, did the signature neck roll, and proceeded with the push-ups before standing to her feet.

Fueled by anger she could have completed a hundred more push-ups. After inspections were complete Aisha and Taylor quickly came to Ava's aid. The girls came to a consensus that Ava's actions were just. Ava knew that her natural curl pattern wasn't viewed as "professional" in the eyes of corporate America. She straightened her hair and still managed to be ridiculed by her Corporal, a white man. Ava believed there was an unwritten law that FORBIDS white men from ever speaking about a black woman's hair in a culturally insensitive manner.

All the recruits returned to the classroom with an awkward silence. Ava had always been viewed as the sweet, gentle, team player who was always smiling. However, that day, all bets were off. The recruits met Ava to the mother fucking "Elise" Singleton.

"Singleton, you were wrong for that." Recruit Bell insinuated, defending the Corporal.

"Girl, bye. He was wrong for talking about this hairdo. Furthermore, if you aren't paying for my hair, your comments and opinions aren't warranted. Thank you, and have a nice day."

The recruits starred in disbelief as Ava stormed out of the classroom to call her mother.

"Ma, this self-proclaimed redneck had the nerve to say my hair looked a hot mess. I blanked out and pushed him out of my way. I'm not too sure if I'm going to have a job come five o'clock."

"Relax, he knows better than talking about a black woman's hair, and if he didn't know he learned today. Don't worry about it." Agni rushed off the phone because her second period students were entering the classroom.

Ava returned to her seat, knowing she had the full support of her mother. Cpl. Price entered the classroom shortly after and requested Ava to step outside with him. The nosey recruits watched Ava exit the room.

"I had no idea I was going to set you off like that, Recruit Singleton."

"Corporal, with all due respect, I used my hard-earned money to get my hair done. I believe your comment was beyond disrespectful."

"You have to understand that criminals and the public are going to say things to upset you, hoping you react. You need to learn how to control yourself. I am sorry that I have offended you. Recruit Singleton, I think you are very beautiful and you remind me of the actress Halle Berry. You could never look a hot mess even if you tried. I just want you to be prepared to deal with people who try to provoke you on the streets."

"I apologize as well." Ava shook Cpl. Price's hand as a peace offering.

See, it didn't matter if the man was a redneck or not. He taught Ava a valuable lesson. A police officer must be able to maintain a certain level of professionalism and not be easily provoked by others. When you allow people to get under your skin, they win the battle. Ava looked at Cpl. Price in a different light after that day. She even caught up to Bell in the locker room and apologized for her earlier behavior, after a lengthy discussion about black hair. The two recruits embraced before completing the daily physical training.

There were no more "angry black woman" moments for Ava throughout the police academy. Even through other trying times, she sported her happy-go-lucky demeanor for all to see. The 34th Police Basic Introductory Class was now down to thirty-five recruits. Seven people had rung the bell. The female recruits bonded with each other as they faced various obstacles together in a predominantly male work force. A middle-aged female training officer frequented the girls' locker room. Primarily to provide short speeches on how the female recruits should conduct themselves.

"Be prepared. There are 900 men in this department. You are all beautiful ladies so expect the rumor mill to say that you are pregnant at least twice. Also, I better not see you wearing anything but black hair bows with your uniform. Anything else is just flat out tacky."

The female training officer stated, standing on top of one of the locker room benches.

Ava translated the tangent "Ladies keep your legs closed and off limits to the men of the police department." Luckily, the jail intake officer was technically a part of the county and worked under the Sheriff.

There were several rumors heard throughout the training center. Many thought Bell and Cpl. Price were having sexual relations. Bell was always in his office, and it was apparent to the recruits that she received extra favoritism. Recruit Candy Man gave out more than candy to two female recruits. In a nut shell, the threesome shared an uncontrollable itch in their groin area, and they could be observed trying to secretly scratch while sitting in the classroom. Ford was dating one of the female officers who served as a role player during the narcotics practicals.

The gossip was childish and reminded Ava of high school. She had managed to stay clear of the rumor mill for the most part. Besides the fact that Owens told Ava he heard she was sleeping with Jones in the men's locker room. Now, Ava and Jones did have a little chemistry, but Ava never crossed any boundaries. There was no way she would ever sleep with a married man; especially one with a wife who was four months pregnant. Ava distanced herself from Jones to uphold her reputation.

The recruits were getting ready for the Use of Force class. They would be tased and maced so they would know how it felt before they utilized the weapons on someone else. The instructors warned the recruits that when some people get tased, they involuntary have bowel leakage. Ava was nervous about the tasing because it was unfamiliar territory. However, mace was almost second nature to her, compliments of too many black people gathering and showing out. One fortunate recruit provided documentation of undergoing Lasik surgery and was excused from being maced.

The day of the tasing quickly arrived. The recruits learned that the taser gun sends 50,000 volts through the body, causing temporary neuromuscular incapacitation. After lunch, each recruit had to be tased if they wanted to carry the weapon on their duty belt. Thanks to budget cuts only two officers would take the probes and the rest of the class would receive a dry stun through clips. Anticipation began to overwhelm Ava who had no appetite for lunch. The possibility of dropping a load in front of her fellow recruits was not going to be an option. Taylor and Ava took a girl's trip to the bathroom with the sole purpose of forcing a bowel movement.

Lunch break was over and the recruits slowly entered the mat room. Ford and Jones were designated to be probe takers. Sgt. Evans stood about ten feet away from Ford who was tased first. The two probes were spread in the upper and lower portion of his back. Ford would have fallen flat on his face if two recruits weren't spotting him. Ava was in-tune to Ford's pain but tried to "play it cool."

Sgt. Evans tased Jones next; one probe landed in the center of his back, but the other probe landed where the sun doesn't shine. Jones the big muscular guy was screaming like he was giving birth to a twelve-pound baby. Ava didn't understand why she put herself in these types of situations. Watching two grown men struggling to mask the pain was less than reassuring. The thought of running out the back door and ringing the bell crossed her mind. *Psalms 119:105, "Your word is a lamp unto my feet and a light to my path."* Ava had no idea what type of lightening was about to strike her path.

Sgt. Evans looked around the mat room, "I need two female volunteers next."

Ava and Taylor reluctantly raised their hands together. "We'll go sir," Ava replied.

He placed the clips on Ava's right shoulder and Taylor's left shoulder. Afterwards, he ordered the duo to sit Indian style on the padded floor.

"The current is going to travel through both of their bodies," Sgt. Evans explained. Ava closed her eyes and prayed that she would make it through the storm.

Sgt. Evans yelled, "Taser! Taser! Taser!"

The pain circulated through Ava's body. First, her right leg began to shake uncontrollably like a bad rendition of the "Stanky Leg." Panicked Ava thought she was having a heart attack.

"Shhhhh-it!" Ava mumbled, hearing the recruits giggling in the background.

Taylor was taking the pain a lot better than Ava, whose left leg had locked out on top of hers. Taylor sat doing a light "Harlem Shake" unbothered. The five second ride with the taser felt like an eternity.

"I said *ship* you guys," Ava stated with clarity after the taser clips had been removed.

The following week the recruits completed the classroom portion of firearms. Ava didn't have any trouble in the classroom, but the gun range was a different story. Sgt. Evans had all the recruits line up against the wall as he pointed a gun in each recruits' face. While looking down the barrel of the gun Ava thought of her favorite bible verse *Isaiah 54:17*, *"No weapon formed against you shall prosper, and every tongue that rises against you in judgment You shall condemn. This is the heritage of the servants of the Lord, and their righteousness is from Me, Says the Lord."*

Her heart rate stayed normal knowing the gun was empty and they were just playing mind games. The command staff wanted the recruits to know how it felt to have a gun pointed in their face in a controlled environment, so they wouldn't freeze up in a potential real-world scenario. The recruits were trained to have a fight mentality and were provided with different techniques to disarm a suspect with a gun.

Let's be clear, Ava was not the person to stand beside with a live weapon locked and loaded. The palms of her hands were constantly sweating and slippery because of the cocoa butter she used to moisturize. She accidently dropped her gun, a Glock 23, while practicing at the gun range on more than one occasion. The firearms instructors were infuriated since she was risking everyone's safety. Cpl. Price brought her a towel after discovering her hands were so sweaty that she couldn't maintain her grip on the gun. The towel was a blessing because she was able to hang on to her gun thereafter.

Now that Ava could hold on to the gun, she had to address her next issue. Poor thing couldn't shoot to save her life. She was shooting the concrete floors and the ceiling more than the target. Ava had never shot a gun before joining the police academy and didn't come from a family of hunters. Hell, she wasn't even sure she needed a gun. At the end of the day, the gun was deadly force and Ava wanted it to be her last option. The thought of taking the life of another human being was gut wrenching. Every time Ava fired her weapon she began to psych herself out mentally. The target helper identified that Ava was anticipating recoil, jerking the trigger, breaking her wrist, and not following through with her shot.

"I don't know what it is, but every black woman has struggled in firearms," a firearms instructor told Ava.

Feeling down, Ava became mute. Maybe it was something in her DNA she thought. Most black women kill people with words anyhow. The day came for the recruits to qualify with their service weapons. Ava and Taylor both failed the course. Taylor passed the state mandated course on her second attempt. Unfortunately, Ava just couldn't figure out how to hit the target, failing at all three attempts.

"Ava, you will have one more final opportunity at the end of the week. If you fail again you will have to wait a year to reapply for police academy." A firearms instructor stated in a composed tone reassuring Ava.

Cpl. Price walked into one of Ava's remediation sessions, "You haven't struggled any up until this point. You have scored in the top 5% of every test you have taken. Do not let me down. I know you can do it."

A defeated Ava nodded her head. The stakes were high. She was going to need several prayers sent up to pass.

"I don't know your religion, but I think that you should fast and pray until your retest," Sgt. Evans suggested.

"I've got to do something Serge," soft-spoken Ava replied.

With no time to spare, she went to the local gun range on her own. She discovered that her aim was most inaccurate from the 15-25-yard line. Nearly all her long-distance shots were going too far left, completely missing the paper target. By aiming to the right of the bullseye a half inch, Ava began to shoot the paper target. She had corrected the issue temporarily and practiced the state qualification course.

On the day of the retest, she was full off the word of God. *Matthew 6:16-18, "Moreover when ye fast, do not be like the hypocrites, with a sad countenance. For they disfigure their faces that they may appear unto men to be fasting. Assuredly, I say to you, they have their reward. But you, when you fast, anoint your head, and wash your face, so that you do not appear to men to be fasting, but to your Father who is in the secret place: and your Father who sees in secret will reward you openly."*

She walked into the gun range knowing the battle was already won.

"How are you feeling this morning?" The firearms instructor asked with a serene smile.

"I'm ready! Let's do it!" Ava replied cheerful.

"Okay, I'm going to reverse the qualification course for you. That way you can get the long-distance portion of the course out the way. How does that sound?"

"Sounds like a plan."

Ava was ready for whatever they threw at her. She would start from the twenty-five-yard line working her way up to the three-yard line. Under time, Ava had only thirty seconds to take five shots standing and five shots in the prone position. After a deep breath, she aimed to the right of the bullseye just like she practiced. By the end of the course, Ava had completely annihilated the red bulls-eye.

The firearms instructor wrote 98% at the top of Ava's target. Sgt. Evans and Cpl. Price embraced her as she walked out of the gun range smiling. The two had been secretly watching Ava qualify. The other recruits were excited once they were notified of her passing. Agni, JaQuan, and Keisha accompanied Ava to a Mexican restaurant that night to celebrate. Ava was blessed to have a good support system made up of family.

The police academy was nearing the end. The recruits went to complete a week of Defensive Driving with the Troopers in Marlboro, North Carolina on their barracks. Throughout the week, the recruits would undertake more vigorous military style training. The recruits were given fifteen minutes to eat all the food on their plates in silence. If any food was leftover, there would be hell to pay. The punishment would be nothing less than extreme physical activity. Thankfully the recruits were no stranger to gluttony.

The recruits got a week off from daily inspections. This was due to the fact, they had to train and successfully complete driving courses for precision, evasive movements, hydroplaning, vehicle pursuit takedowns, and more. Ava had been driving her grandpa's truck on the back-country roads since the age of seven.

Empowered, Ava sat behind the wheel of the oversized Ford Crown Victoria. Unable to see over the steering wheel, Ava made a booster seat out of a pillow. On the precision course, Ava redeemed herself by not displacing any orange cones.

"You from the hood ain't you? That's the only way you learn how to drive like that." A black State Trooper asked.

"No sir. I'm just a country girl," Ava smiled continuing to set the bar high for the other recruits.

Driving on the race tracks brought the recruits closer together. One night they snuck off the barracks for some good ole laser tag. It was the most fun Ava had since joining the academy. She no longer felt like a robot but an actual human. Above all, Ava realized her academy class consisted of honorable men and women who wanted to serve and protect the Minor Hills community.

The recruits prepared to graduate on a cold rainy day. They had returned the mall security cop uniforms back into logistics and were now wearing the official black police uniforms. The 34th Police Basic Introductory Class looked like a force to be reckoned with. The recruits were moments away from being sworn police officers. At this point, all the recruits were acting like their shit didn't stink.

Sgt. Evans told the recruits, "Whatever you do, please don't drop the Bible."

A sworn officer demonstrated how the recruits should hold their bibles in unison. They were to hold the bibles in their left hand, with their thumb on the bottom of the book, and the other four fingers on top. The right hand was to be held over their heart. The recruits marched out on stage in alphabetical order. Ava was already struggling to maintain the grip of the bible. Her miniature cocoa butter hands were still sweating. Her family, friends, and sorority sisters had driven across the Carolina's for her big day. Cpl. Price was halfway through the Police Officer's Oath when it happened.

"Booom!" Ava dropped the Holy Bible.

Ava's hands just couldn't handle the task of holding the bible in that position for over five minutes. She quickly picked the Bible with the slight concealment of standing in the second row. Finally, he finished reading the Oath and began calling the names of the newly sworn police officers. Since Ava dropped her Bible she questioned being sworn in.

"Officer Ava Elise Singleton." Cpl. Price announced with a large smile.

A relieved Ava walked across the stage gracefully shaking hands with The Chief, Sgt. Evans, and Cpl. Price. At the end of the stage stood Agni, JaQuan, and Keisha. Agni pinned Ava's badge #246, on the left side of her uniform covering her heart. Officer Singleton was in the house.

CHAPTER 4

FIELD TRAINING

"You have been pretending to be a police officer for the past few months. Now it's time to see what you are made of." Field Training Officer Leduc stated throwing Ava the keys.

Speechless, Ava began to complete the daily inspection with a solitary smile affixed.

"They would give me someone who smiles all the time," Leduc sneered.

Ava ignored Leduc's comments as she was not going to let anyone break her spirit. She felt that he should have started the conversation off with a proper introduction, "Nice to meet you. How are you doing today?"

Leduc changed his demeanor and became more personable realizing his foolery had no effect on Ava.

"I am the father of a newborn baby girl named Savannah. Sorry, if I came off like a dick. My wife is currently not employed and the bills are flowing in. I also don't believe in God. I hope that is not a problem."

"Why don't you believe in God?" Ava inquired, not having many prior interactions with non-believers.

"If there was a God why would he allow small children to be executed with a Kalashnikov better known as an AK- 47 or "chopper?" I held a two-year-old boy as he took his last breath on earth. I checked and couldn't find a pulse on his sisters. The children were innocent victims who lost their lives due to domestic violence in the home. I had never cried on this job until that day."

"Damn, that's sad." Ava tried to console Leduc by patting him on the shoulder. Who could bear the thought of watching a child take their last breath?

Deep down Ava knew that all things work together for the greater good. However, the greater good in that situation was beyond her understanding. Unlike some Christians, she didn't believe in pushing her views on others. Ava was the opposite of Aunt Sally in the movie *Fighting Temptations.* She would just have to let her light shine bright. *Matthew 5:16,* *"Let your light so shine before men, that they may see your good works, and glorify your Father in heaven."*

After an uncomfortable silence, Ava suggested to Leduc, "Let's go answer some calls."

"Good idea, let's see if you learned anything in the academy. We are car "3-3-6" by the way."

She began to write his earlier behavior off as him being a city boy from up north. Leduc had been a part of a hockey team in high school with the specific task of roughing up the players on the other team.

Ava began driving the patrol vehicle around in circles thinking about the long twelve-hour shift ahead. The thought of stopping a car crossed her mind, but she didn't want to choke over the radio. She figured that waiting to be dispatched would be her best option. However, Leduc had other plans.

"Why can we stop that truck?"

Without hesitation, Ava replied, "The left headlight is out and they are failing to maintain their lane." She got the hint he wanted her to stop the truck.

"Interesting," he said while shrugging his shoulders.

The truck was swerving in and out of the travel lane posing a threat to general motorists. After a deep breath, she keyed up on the radio, "Car 3-3-6 I'll be 10-38."

"Car 3-3-6 go head."

"I'll be at…..." Silence, Ava did not know her location.

"We are at Highland and Fourth. Out with North Carolina Registration, Delta-Bravo-Oscar-X-X-X-X on a blue Ford F-150 occupied by one." Leduc spoke up.

"Copy," communications acknowledged.

To redeem herself, Ava made a tactical passenger side approach on the vehicle with her left hand holding her flashlight. Since she was a right-handed shooter, she wanted to be able to quickly draw her service weapon.

"Excuse me sir, license and registration please." Ava asked

looking at the empty beer bottles and plastic red SOLO® Cup in the center console. Leduc stood back spectating.

"No, sorry." The man responded handing Ava a Mexican passport, identifying himself as Carlos Ramos. He had glossy eyes and a strong odor of alcohol emanating from his person.

"Sir, I need you to step out of the vehicle."

Mr. Ramos was short in stature, mildly obese, and had a light sandy colored skin tone. He slowly stepped out of the vehicle, holding on to the door frame to maintain his balance. Mr. Ramos was wearing a navy-blue t-shirt, khaki cargo pants, and a pair of construction work boots. There was a wet spot to the right of his zipper that was halfway down.

"What is that wet spot on your pants?" Ava asked knowing he had pissed on himself.

"I fucking party hard mi amiga, muchas cervezas." Mr. Ramos replied pleasantly.

He is probably going to jail, Ava thought grabbing the Portable Breath Test (PBT).

"My friend, I need you to blow into this straw for me."

Mr. Ramos took a deep breath and blew into the PBT that measured his blood alcohol content at 0.24, three times the legal limit.

Testing positive for alcohol in his system she began to conduct the Standardized Field Sobriety Tests.

"Mr. Ramos, do you have any medical condition that may prevent you from following my finger, walking in a straight line, or standing on one leg for approximately thirty seconds?"

"No," he replied unconcerned.

"I'm going to start with the Horizontal Gaze Nystagmus Test. I need you to keep your head straight and follow my finger with your eyes." Mr. Ramos could not follow Ava's finger without moving his entire head.

"Next, I need you to complete the Walk and Turn Test. Please stand heel to toe with your hands to the side, while I demonstrate the instructions." Mr. Ramos struggled to maintain the correct stance.

Ava counted aloud, "One...two...and so on" taking nine heel-to-toe steps down on an imaginary line. She then made a small prescribed turn and took the last nine heel-to-toe steps back, while continuing to count.

"Do you have any questions?" Mr. Ramos shook his head and began walking. His first few steps looked like he was walking across hot lava standing on his tippy toes. Mr. Ramos then raised his arms out like an airplane to balance.

After taking twenty steps, he asked, "Can I do the next test? I no good at this."

"Yes, we can do that. Stand still with your feet together. Do not move until you have been further instructed to do so. I'm going to demonstrate the One Leg Stand Test for you."

Ava held one leg approximately six inches from the ground with her arms to her side. Counting aloud, "One thousand one, one thousand two...," for about thirty seconds.

"Do you understand Mr. Ramos?" Placing her leg down in relief.

"Yes," lifting his left leg up an inch before immediately putting it back down.

He attempted to complete the test again, hoping for better luck with his right leg. While raising his right leg, he lost his balance and nearly fell to the ground.

Leduc caught Mr. Ramos, "You are responsible for him while he is in your custody, Singleton."

Knowing that he might cause bodily harm to himself, she ended the test.

"Mr. Ramos, I need you to turn around and place your hands behind your back. You are under arrest for Driving While Impaired." First night on the job and she had finally made use of her shiny new handcuffs.

While being transported to the Minor Hills Jail Mr. Ramos uttered, "I don't care what you all have in store for me. My girl is going to kill me!"

"Hopefully she is not too hard on you Mr. Ramos." Ava stated driving into the sally port.

Ludec was a certified Chemical Analyst and administered the chemical test on Mr. Ramos. He blew a 0.24 followed by a 0.25 in the intoxilyzer room. Mr. Ramos was charged with Failing to Maintain Lane, Failing to Burn Headlamps, and Driving While Impaired. He stood before the magistrate where he received a written promise to appear.

"You did pretty good," Leduc was truly impressed.

"Yes, I know." A self-assured Ava replied.

"A lot of people hate dealing with drunk drivers because of the amount of paperwork. However, the paperwork is only a formality and it beats responding to a fatality any day. In Minor Hills we have had 10 people killed by drunk drivers in the last year. Drinking and driving is something we don't cut breaks on. Now let's see what else this night has to offer."

Being raised in a household with an alcoholic Ava didn't mind the extra paperwork. While returning to the patrol vehicle, police communications requested the assistance of any available female officer.

Ava spoke up, "Car 3-3-6."

"I need you to respond to 6254 Woodland Avenue to assist with a traffic stop."

"Copy," Ava sensed she just volunteered herself for a strip search.

A lost Ava broke out her smartphone so she could listen to the automated voice directions in lieu of the programmed mapping system on her rugged computer. Upon arriving on scene, officers told her that they had found a large sum of money, marijuana, and a digital scale. They also let her know that notorious drug dealer, "Red," was inside the vehicle.

A plain clothes male officer asked Ava, "Can you please transport the female to a restroom and complete a strip search. She has a lengthy history of prostitution and narcotics."

"Sure. Is her name Christen Richards?"

"Yes," stated the officer handing Ava her North Carolina photo identification card.

Christen Richards was a white female with skin the color of cauliflower. Anyone with a brain would have thought she was pushing forty. Her license indicated that she was twenty-seven years of age, but the drugs had aged her out. She couldn't weigh more than ninety pounds and her short brown wiry hair was untamed. Christen was wearing a dingy tank top, holey light blue jeans, and some tennis shoes that should have been retired ten years ago. Despite having burned lips, chronic cotton mouth, with an overgrown unibrow, Ava could tell that she was once a beautiful lady. However, crack had gotten the best of her.

Christen told Ava, "Honey, I turn tricks and suck dick in pursuit of my next fix. That fucking pig has it out for me." Ava could only shake her head.

Leduc and Ava walked Christen towards the mini mart.

Officer Leduc stood outside the restroom, "If you act stupid with Officer Singleton, all bets are off and I will be forced to come in for officer safety."

Ava put on her latex gloves, in preparation for the strip search. The claustrophobic restroom composed of a mirror, toilet, and a trash can put Ava on the fast track.

"Christen do you have any needles or pipes that may poke me or illegal drugs on your person?"

"I have a crack rock in my bra and I am on my period. I didn't use a tampon or a pad because I spent my last few dollars on the rock. Just to give you the heads up, I stink. Sorry," she replied acting nonchalant.

"Um...Thank you for the warning." Ava struggled to utter the words while masking her discontent.

"Christen, I'm going to have you remove each article of your clothing. Please pass me your shirt."

Christen handed the shirt to Ava who checked it for contraband across every seam.

The shirt was good, "I need you to pass me your bra."

"Here you go," Christen stated removing the crack rock from her bra.

"Thank you," Ava replied placing the drugs in the evidence bag.

While searching the bra, Ava located a hole in the under wiring, containing three heroin bindles.

"Why didn't you tell me about the heroin?" Ava scowled, insulted as she placed the drugs in the evidence bag.

"I thought there was a chance you wouldn't find it, Rookie. Look, I got addicted to heroin trying to ditch crack."

"I told you from the beginning if you had anything illegal let me know. I can't trust you don't have anything else on you. Put your shirt and bra back on."

"Come on! I couldn't tell you everything I'm holding."

Ava directed Christen to remove her tennis shoes and socks. A folded dollar fell out of the left sock. Next, she removed her jeans that held a secret compartment behind the zipper. Inside the compartment, Ava collected a burnt glass pipe with copper shavings. The common drug paraphernalia found with crack users.

"Remove your panties," Ava requested.

Christen slid her dirty brown panties down her legs. She had a makeshift pad of a few pieces of cheap toilet tissue inside her panties. The restroom suddenly smelled like a blood bank inside a fish market.

"Here you go," attempting to hand Ava her panties.

Not wanting to smell the funk Ava shook her head "no." She was fine visually inspecting the panties from a distance. After studying Human Papillomavirus (HPV), Human Immunodeficiency Virus (HIV), and other sexually transmitted diseases at the collegiate level, there was no way in H-E-L-L Ava was going to touch those panties. Being a police woman had to be more than strip searching prostitutes on their periods with stained panties. There was one last place to check.

"Going to need you to bend over, touch your toes, and spread your cheeks." Christen complied while Ava held her breath like an Olympic diver, taking a quick peek.

It had to be checked to make sure no illegal drugs or weapons were concealed in her "natural pockets." Finished with the search, she immediately had Christen put her clothes back on before placing her in handcuffs. Ava was unaware that the officers outside had placed bets on whether or not she would find the dope. Clueless, Ava escorted Christen out of the restroom.

"Hey guys, were you looking for this?" Ava held up the evidence bag of crack rocks, heroin bindles, and drug paraphernalia.

The officers thanked Ava and took custody of Christen and the drugs.

"I know that sucked," Leduc laughed.

"I should have yelled HELP! That way you could of ran in and smelled the funk."

"Not if you want to pass field training."

The jokes didn't last very long as the emergency tones blasted through the portable and car radio.

"Car 3-3-6 and Car 3-5-6 we got shots fired in the area of Minor Hills Inn, located at 4206 Broad St."

"En-route," both units advised communications.

"We are receiving multiple calls. One male subject down, suffering from a gunshot wound to the chest."

"Copy, we will be responding emergency traffic," Officer Leduc cautioned.

Ava jumped in the driver's seat, activating her emergency lights and sirens. In less than ten seconds she had accelerated from 0 to 70 mph. Within twenty-two seconds she was traveling over 100 mph. The adrenaline was running through Ava's body and her heart rate exceeded the normal resting rate. Ava's sweaty palms could barely grip the steering wheel.

All her life she heard, "Police take longer to respond to black neighborhoods."

Ava was determined that was not going to be the case.

"We are not going to be any good to anybody if we don't make it to the call alive," Leduc stated making a valid point.

Starting to lose control, Ava began to ease off the gas. The Minor

Hills Inn was only a couple of blocks away. Turning off her siren and blue lights for a more tactical approach. The reality of seeing someone suffering from a gunshot wound to the chest was setting in.

There were approximately a hundred young adults in the parking lot when Ava arrived on scene. They had gathered for Shante's eighteenth birthday party where a small dispute led to gunfire erupting. The victim was laying down in the breezeway, covered in his own vomit. Two officers were administering first aid. On crowd control duty, Ava was unable to get a close look at the victim. The paramedics came in and immediately took over cardiopulmonary resuscitation. Undecided if she wanted to see the victim up close, Ava ran and grabbed the crime scene tape to appear busy.

Officer Leduc asked, "Did you see the victim?"

"No, I was helping to secure the scene." She replied being partially honest.

Leduc walked Ava to the ambulance where she had a full view of the victim, Rayshawn Hall.

Leduc whispered, "Ava, he is dead. The crowd has the propensity to act violently towards first responders. EMS wants to provide the appearance they are doing everything they can for the victim to keep the peace."

Mr. Hall was wearing a red t-shirt and blue jeans. His shirt had been cut open by the first responders administering aid. The blood had seeped down to his feet saturating the lower limbs. The body begun going through algor mortis, the "death chill." The young man had recently turned eighteen and was the father of a two-year old son. Now he was lying on a gurney. Ava felt like she was watching *First 48* up close. Bowing her head, she prayed for the victim's family and a peace of mind. She had never witnessed a dead body any other place than a funeral home. Mr. Hall was officially pronounced dead at 0200 hours, while being transported to the hospital.

After a few short interviews with witnesses on scene, Ava determined that Mr. Hall was executed amongst his peers because he looked at someone the wrong way. The funny thing about respect is, those who don't have it always want to demand it. Presumably the shooter must have skipped over *Philippians 2:3, "Let nothing be done through selfish ambition and conceit, but in lowliness of mind let each esteem others better than himself."*

Still on scene, a superior officer directed Ava to complete the "rookie task" of maintaining the crime scene log. She had to write down the name and time any first responder entered or exited the scene. Ava had a lack of appetite standing outside of the patrol vehicle with the crime scene log in hand. Less than eight hours into the shift, the combination of a prostitute's dirty panties and the disregard of human life was overwhelming.

Ava managed to stay in "professional mode" until her old academy mate, Bell relieved her at 0630 hours. She crawled into her empty bed and popped open a bottle of Moscato, hoping the alcohol would ease the stresses of the day. She tossed and turned the next couple of nights, replaying images of the deceased Mr. Hall in her head. Also, the thought of another young black child being raised without a father weighed heavily on Ava's soul. Realizing the alcohol was not aiding, Ava turned to the source, GOD. Undoubtedly, through prayer, Ava found peace and serenity.

The next twelve weeks of training with Leduc were a breeze. He was glad his first trainee had a college education. Successfully completing the first phase of training, Ava prepared to enter the evaluation phase with Field Training Officer Mack. While waiting in the line-up room, Officer Mack walked by partially dressed carrying a gym bag. Mack was a black male, approximately fifty-four years of age, 5'6, weighing 175 pounds. He had over twenty years of policing experience, was a former marine, and mechanical engineer by trade. He returned to the line-up room and introduced himself.

"Hello, Officer Singleton. You have me for the next couple of weeks for your evaluation phase. Just so you know, before we actually start answering calls we must get coffee every day."

Ava giggled, "Yes sir."

Inside she was praying that she would be released for solo assignment on time and not require additional training. One night after the daily coffee run she was dispatched to a burglary of residence at an off-campus housing unit. The victim, Charlotte Brown advised that she returned home from the library and noticed that her front door was unsecured. Ms. Brown reported her 32-inch flat screen television, laptop computer, and $20.00 cash had been stolen. Ava walked around the first story apartment and determined the point of entry was the bedroom window. Taking initiative, Ava requested a Crime Scene Investigator to process the crime scene. The bitter thought of someone stealing from an innocent college student was discerning for Ava.

The Crime Scene Investigator (CSI) arrived and asked to borrow Ava's Maglite to take pictures of the apartment door. While CSI was taking pictures, Ava observed a suspicious subject walking behind the apartments towards Ms. Brown's residence. The subject was a dark skinned black male, mid-thirties, slim build, mini-afro, approximately 5'3 with a snaggletooth. The subject was drinking a "forty" with the signature brown bag in his right hand. The man looked like he was carrying a screwdriver in his left hand. He was wearing a black hoody, dark jeans, and boots.

"I'm not a betting woman, but if I was, I'd bet he isn't a student at anybody's college," Ava stated.

"Hmm, well go talk to him," Mack replied in a monotonous voice.

Standing approximately forty yards away from the suspicious subject she yelled, "Excuse me, sir!" The guy made eye contact with Ava and continued walking as if she didn't exist. Ava began walking towards the subject.

Again she yelled with more authority, "Excuse me sir!"

The subject looked around and asked, "Who me?" He then threw the "forty" down and took off running.

Ava yelled on the radio, "Got a subject running. Start us some cars!"

In her first foot pursuit, the extra thirty-pound equipment took its toll. Winded and fatigued she managed to tell police communications the last direction of travel for the subject. Mack bolted past her, but he soon lost visual of the subject. It was a dark night with many places to hide.

"What happened girl? You just let an old man out run you."

"Shut up! I know you take those extra special blue pills, Grandpa! That's the only way you got an extra boost."

Stepping up, Ava assigned several patrol cars to the surrounding area. With enough units forming a perimeter, she knew the subject would be forced to lay down. The handsome Canine Officer Wells came to the rescue with his dark hair, bronzed skin, hazel eyes, and K-9 Ziggy. Ziggy was a mature German Shephard that weighed in at a hundred pounds. He was not only known for his big bark but also his big bite. They hit the ground running with Ava following loosely behind them for back-up. Ziggy began tracking northeast towards the Rib Spot. Realizing Ziggy was sidetracked, Wells refocused his attention. Ziggy crossed the railroad track and stopped at some thorn bushes barking viciously. The hormone epinephrine was released in Ava's body. This caused her glucose levels to rise, fueling an added level of alertness, and a second wind.

Wells began giving loud verbal commands, "Come out with your hands up! If not, I will let my dog pull you out!"

"Coming out man. I got all these thorns on me," a male voice jeered.

A man covered in thorns slowly came out of the bushes. Ava identified the man as the same individual who ran from her. He was uncooperative, intoxicated, and provided a fictitious name of "Bishop Smith." She transported him down to the Minor Hills jail and identified him using the fingerprinting system. The suspicious subject was identified as Kentrell Cole who had sixteen active warrants for Breaking and Entering and Probation Violations. Later, CSI linked Mr. Cole's fingerprints to Ms. Brown's campus apartment. He was held under a $120,000 bond. Ava saw full circle the benefits of teamwork, taking a menace to society off the streets.

"Officer Singleton you performed well tonight. I mean they don't allow me to take off points for your running, so I will recommend the Captain release you for solo assignment immediately."

"Thanks, old man. You're not too bad yourself."

CHAPTER 5

MISSES OFFICER

Ava had been assigned to "Southwest Squad S." The graveyard shift that would force her to see the sun set and rise every workday. Senior officers jumped at the chance to leave night shift amidst the new officers being released for solo assignment. The Southwest Division statistically answered 75% of the calls in Minor Hills. The division consisted of four housing projects, a trailer park, several residential neighborhoods, and a shopping center.

The thought of being the only rookie on a squad was not appealing. Ava understood that her mishaps would be magnified going through the "rookie" rite of passage. Ava was instantly relieved after learning Jones had been assigned to the same squad. The pressure of holding her own in a male dominated workforce was stressful enough. The two sat nervously waiting to meet the officers of Southwest Squad S in the line-up room. It was a small SMART classroom equipped with nine tables, twelve swivel chairs, a 60" television, and a white board. The television had been confiscated from a drug dealer's house during a raid. Ava was taking everything in, knowing she would meet in the room before starting any duty day on patrol. Officers Bixby and Stewart came strolling in together.

"Here ye, Here ye. Welcome aboard to Southwest Squad S ladies and gentlemen." Officer Bixby stated in an animated voice.

"Thank you, sir." Ava and Jones replied.

Officer Bixby was attractive until he opened his completely unfiltered mouth. Bixby was approximately 6'4, olive skin, early twenties, athletic build, and tapered dark black hair. His black boots had turned a hunter green and could no longer withstand shoe polish. Bixby's body language very much exuded an "I don't give a fuck" vibe.

On the other hand, Stewart came from a military background and was strictly by the book. He was a young white male, approximately 5'7, buzz-cut blonde hair, and a noticeable beer belly. Stewart's shoes were freshly polished at the toe portion. His uniform was professionally pressed with crisp creases going down each arm sleeve and pant leg. Stewart was the golden boy favorited amongst the command staff. He received strict orders from the higher-ups to keep Bixby on a short leash. The two reminded Ava of the American animated television series *Pinky and the Brain*.

A female officer walked in and sat at a table. She made eye contact with all but spoke to no one. Her name was Officer Lynn. She was a mysterious young white female with long brown hair. Next, Officer Quinn entered the room with swag in his steps, reminiscent of

President Barack Obama. He was a dark-skinned brother from Philadelphia with a laid-back demeanor. He shook hands with Ava and Jones.

Lastly, Sergeant Turner and Corporal Wallace walked in with stripes, more specifically chevrons, decorating their arms. Sgt. Turner had a reputation of being called "Turn Them Loose Turner" because he couldn't catch a criminal in a wheelchair. Many heard through the grapevine that he was a terrible supervisor just riding off nepotism's privilege. The whole police department was aware of the Turner lineage. Sgt. Turner was approximately forty-five, tall, skinny build, brown hair, and a raspy voice compliments of chain smoking.

Cpl. Wallace was a stereotypical older white man in his mid-fifties. He didn't necessarily believe women should work in law enforcement and Ava could read it all over his face. There was a negative aura that surrounded him. Rumors traveled that Cpl. Wallace was bitter because he could never get promoted pass Corporal. The man spent a lot of time making other officers miserable. They gave him the nickname, "Report Nazi" because he always denied reports for simple errors.

Sgt. Turner welcomed Ava and Jones to Southwest Squad S. He then began reading the Minor Hill's 24-Hour Summary Report. "One hundred and twelve calls answered, thirty-six arrests, fourteen citations issued, two uses of force, and ten traffic accidents."

Photographs of Minor Hill's Most Wanted Felons circulated throughout the room. Ava examined the names and photographs in-depth just in case she came across them in the community. Sgt.

Turner dismissed the squad.

Ava loaded up her police equipment in the front passenger's seat, relieved the space would no longer be occupied with a Field Training Officer. She joined forces with Jones ready to hit the beat, since no calls of service were holding. The two began surveillance on a local mom and pop shop notorious for drug activity and prostitution. Five minutes into the operation, a hand-to-hand transaction between two black males was observed. With no real plan of action, they both ran up to the store on foot. At the same time, one of the males involved jumped into a car fleeing the area, while the second subject ditched his dope. Needless to say, their first attempt at being drug cops was an epic fail. However, they learned from their rookie mistakes. To complete a successful stake-out and take-down, they would need at least four officers. Stewart and Bixby stopped by.

"You really shouldn't watch the store unless you have asked the zone cars for permission," an offended Stewart stated.

Ava replied, "My badge says Minor Hills Police Department, not Minor Hills Police Department Go Ask Zone Cars Permission. I will go any and everywhere I please in this city to enforce the criminal laws I swore to uphold. Furthermore, if you guys have a problem with someone addressing criminal activity in your zone, you may have a bigger issue." Jones stood holding the collars of his shirt down to control himself.

The reality was Ava didn't even know the locality of her zone. However, she was not going to allow them to think that she was a pushover. She knew they were being territorial and didn't want them to get a good bust in their drug infested zone.

Communications dispatched Ava to a noise disturbance call regarding barking dogs. Ava drove around in circles trying to locate the address. Finally, she pulled over to use the navigation system on her smart phone.

"I see you been en-route to the noise disturbance call for twenty minutes. You are literally two minutes away." Stewart sent Ava a message through the mobile communications terminal. Irritated, Ava ignored Stewart who could have chosen to help her twenty minutes ago. By the time she arrived on scene, the dogs had fallen asleep. Ava found solace in knowing that her paycheck would not be deducted for being directionally challenged.

As time passed, the racial divide on Southwest Squad S became more and more obvious to Ava. Yet again, she observed de facto segregation taking place during meal times. However, if an officer ever requested assistance, race was put on the backburner. Every officer would drop what they were doing to assist. The officers were a part of something greater, the thin Blue Line outlined in black, representing the strong bond of the law enforcement community. The Blue Line commemorated the fallen law enforcement officers, the duty of law enforcement to protect the community, and the daily risk of death an officer faces.

Sadly, a dark cloud of misfortune seemingly floated over the community. Ava's fellow recruit Ford had been hit by a drunk driver after being released for solo assignment. A retired corporal had been diagnosed with throat cancer and would be having a portion of his tongue removed. A popular young high school athlete collapsed during football practice and was in critical condition. Minor Hills was struck with many tragedies in a short amount of time. Befittingly, the police secretary sent out a departmental email detailing the events of an upcoming service prayer. The event was scheduled at the Police Plaza for law enforcement and the community to uplift each other during the trying times.

Ava went to the prayer service with her original academy crew Aisha and Taylor. The lady cops dressed in their Class A uniforms which included their uniformed shirt, black tie, slick pants, and shiny high gloss police shoes. They were joined outside the Police Plaza with over a hundred officers and members of the community. The atmosphere was extremely uplifting as the crowd was filled with prayer warriors who rebuked the spirit of calamity and called forth God's peace and angels of protection.

The police secretary thanked everyone for attending and begin reading *Matthew 18:20*, *"For where two or three are gathered together in My name, I am there in the midst of them."*

The crowd interlocked hands after being directed to hold a moment of silence.

Thereafter, the Police Chaplain walked to the podium, "Good Afternoon. Let's bow our heads Minor Hills. Dear Heavenly Father which art in heaven, we have gathered in your name to pray for these officers and members of our community who have been recently affected by tragedy or misfortune. Please touch their bodies, heal them, and send them to the road of recovery. We know that despite what the doctors say, You can make a way if it's Your will and we thank You. Amen."

Once the ceremony ended, the ladies went to lunch at a hidden gem specializing in chicken and waffles. It turns out that Aisha had been dating an EMS Paramedic she met online. Many people on her squad complained because she was busy following behind her boyfriend instead of working her beat. Taylor and Ava of course were still single. They tried dating, but most of the men of Minor Hills weren't hitting on too much. Their love life was drier than the Sahara Desert. Taylor decided that she would start taking Ava out to the professional football games. Since the games were a playground of men, Ava felt obliged to take her up on the offer. Sort of like Neapolitan ice cream filled with money makers, money takers, and money fakers. The ladies continued to gossip over their fair share of mimosas before calling it a night.

The next morning, Southwest Squad S reported to the Minor Hills Court house for their scheduled court date. The officers were required to wear Class A uniforms or business attire. Ava decided to wear her form fitting dress pants and a red cardigan. Glancing in the mirror, Ava noticed her "badonkadonk" was unconcealable. Even though she was blessed with what her mama gave her, Ava truly believed her attire was professional. Contrarily, Cpl. Wallace did not feel the same and wanted Sgt. Turner to address Ava's professionalism the next duty day. Blindsided, Ava was asked to stop by the office after line up.

"Hey! So, you wanted me to stop by?" Ava asked puzzled.

Sgt. Turner closed the door, "Have a seat. Cpl. Wallace brought it to my attention that your clothes were not professional for court yesterday."

"Per the women's etiquette guide, I was dressed in the proper business attire."

"Well, we think your pants were too tight," Cpl. Wallace advised in a contemptuous snort.

"Sorry that you feel that way. I will wear my police uniform for future court dates since you all obviously aren't used to seeing a grown woman with a figure." Ava stood up and dismissed herself from the office.

She went to her patrol vehicle and called Agni knowing the snakes attempt to break her spirit was unwarranted.

"Ma, the Corporal and Sergeant had the nerve to say my clothes were too tight. You've seen my dress pants and have even borrowed them for work. They are always trying to find something wrong with me. I guess they're just mad because their wives don't have no ass!"

"Why are they always picking on you? You got that ass from your mama and you better be proud of it. You document everything they say to you in case you need it later. Let their comments roll off your back like water on a duck."

Self-aware, Ava knew they feared having an educated black woman on the squad. Agni was right, she didn't have time to worry about her supervisors because the Minor Hills community needed her service.

After doing some self-reflection, Ava remembered being happy while volunteering in college. After rekindling that memory, Ava began volunteering at Minor Hills Elementary. There she taught the first grade class leadership skills, teamwork, mathematics, and public safety. Apart from that, Ava loved participating in Christmas with Cops, bringing joy to less fortunate children annually. The children cherished Ava dearly. When they saw her shopping around town, they would often break out in a full sprint to embrace her.

The Minor Hills Police Department was restructuring to focus on neighborhood oriented policing that had been implemented in bigger cities. They began allowing officers to volunteer within the community during duty days. Thus, Ava opted to go on a back-to-school shopping spree with the kids. She was paired with Rakeem, a 2nd grader from the projects. The volunteers and children loaded the old yellow school bus for the journey to the shopping center. Ava could immediately tell that Rakeem was very outgoing. He was the youngest of six children being raised by a single mother.

"Hey, I have to wear uniforms to school now."

"Why is that?" Ava asked.

"Cuz of the gangs," Rakeem replied jokingly. Ava hated the gangs influence on the youth.

"What is your favorite subject?" She asked quickly changing the subject.

"I like math."

"Awesome! My mom is a math teacher. So, what do you want to be when you grow up?"

"I want to be a rapper or a ball player."

"What are you going to do if that doesn't work out for you?"

"I'm going to run track," Rakeem replied as if it was a no brainer.

The bus arrived at the store and with uncontainable excitement, Rakeem was jumping out of his seat ready to shop.

"I only wear boxer briefs, colorful socks, and skinny leg jeans." Rakeem explained.

Ava laughed suspecting that he had a fashionable older brother at the house. She hadn't come across many young boys that cared about their clothing. After Rakeem got the required clothes for school she allowed him to pick out some outfits for the weekend. Rakeem modeled his skinny leg jeans and polo shirt like no other. Ava gave Rakeem everything he wished for. After shopping, they delighted in buttered popcorn and red slushies until it was time for everyone to load the bus. When no one was looking she slipped him a $20.00 bill. Ava gave him a friendly reminder on the importance of receiving an education and staying out of trouble. Volunteering helped Ava forget the stresses of work and put her in brighter spirits.

The racial divide was short lived on Southwest Squad S thanks to Sgt. Turner moving to the morning shift. He was replaced with the newly promoted Sergeant Fitzpatrick. Sgt. Fitzpatrick was a middle aged white man with a charismatic personality. He had worked in Vice Narcotics for over eight years. Under his leadership, the squad began to work together on special assignments, partake in breakfast together, and build more personal relationships. Ava admired the man more for his personal attributes than his drug stats. Being able to bring the squad together in less than a week was remarkable; he was able to do what Sgt. Turner hadn't done, and he'd been there for years. Sgt. Fitzpatrick and his wife adopted a beautiful young daughter from Ethiopia. She was their pride and joy. Not only was Sgt. Fitzpatrick a great commander, but a God-fearing family man as well.

Sgt. Fitzpatrick pushed the squad to seek additional training whenever the opportunity was provided. Ava loved his mindset of betterment. Again, Agni raised her to believe that the only thing in the world that can't be taken away from you is your education. Ava enrolled and attended a Drug Investigation Course designed to help the basic patrol officer. She knew that her drug stats would absolutely have to increase, after the department spent money for her to attend training. Soon after successfully completing the class, Ava was getting drug busts left and right like a pro.

In mid-August, while on routine patrol, Ava observed a vehicle blow past a four way stop sign at a high rate of speed. Moments prior, elementary school children were riding their scooters in the street. Ava keyed up on the radio.

"Car 2-4-6 I will be 10-38."

"Go ahead Car 2-4-6."

"Boars Creek at Juniper St., out with North Carolina Registration Delta-Alpha-Charlie-X- X-X-X on a silver Cadillac."

"Copy."

Ava tactically approached the car on the passenger side, smelling the strong odor of unburned marijuana. When the driver rolled down the passenger window she knew something wasn't quite right.

Policing on the job for only a year Ava caught on fast, gaining an undocumented sixth sense. Uneasy, she requested an assist officer to start her way. Ava knew that she was dealing with more than just "personal usage" marijuana from the driver, Malik Moss. Mr. Moss was dark skinned, articulate, medium build, approximately thirty years of age with a fresh fade. He was wearing a collared shirt, fitted blue jeans, and loafers. Ava could see his carotid artery jumping uncontrollably. In the drug interdiction course Ava learned how the carotid artery moves involuntarily, when a person is under stress.

"Misses Officer please gives me a break ma'am." Mr. Moss stated in a smooth voice reaching under his driver's seat. Apprehensive, Ava removed her gun from her holster.

"Don't reach! Place your hands-on top of the steering wheel! If you don't, Mr. Moss you are a breath away from being the tin man!" Ava yelled loudly pointing her gun at the center mass of Mr. Moss. He slowly moved his hands up to the steering wheel.

"Have my assist step it up to emergency traffic," she told communications.

Ava held Mr. Moss at gunpoint knowing that with drugs came guns. She knew that people's hands are what kill people. Ava knew she was in control since she could see his hands. Her heart steadily raced listening to the police sirens in the distance.

Mr. Moss spontaneously uttered, "Misses Officer, I'm sorry. I only have some weed on me. Please work with me ma'am." While the tears streamed down his face, Ava's anxiety grew.

"I'll see what I can do for you, but don't move." Ava replied with her finger outside the trigger guard.

Cpl. Wallace was the first to arrive on scene. This was the only time Ava could account being reprieved to see him. At Ava's direction, Cpl. Wallace instructed Mr. Moss to step out of the vehicle. He was searched with probable cause and placed in handcuffs. Ava began searching the vehicle as Cpl. Wallace stood by with Mr. Moss.

She started with the driver's seat to see what Mr. Moss had been reaching for. A brown bag containing ninety-four grams of marijuana was under the seat. The marijuana had been packaged into different size bags for the consumer. Some of the weed had even been grinded. In the center console, $1,600.00 cash in small denominations was seized. Underneath the passenger seat was a gunmetal aluminum pocket knife with a four-inch blade. Mr. Moss began sweating profusely after Ava placed the brown bag and knife on top of the car. Upon opening the glove box, Ava located a black handgun under the car manual. Her heart dropped and reality set in that she didn't have the safest profession. After dropping the magazine and taking the round out of the chamber, Ava visually inspected the gun to ensure it was clear.

Bixby and Stewart arrived on scene.

"How do you always get so lucky?" Stewart asked impressed.

"It's not luck, just skill," Ava replied jokingly.

"I'm a little bit jealous; you always stop the right car. Hell, I'm certain that joker would have run away from me." Stewart had heard about the drug bust from Cpl. Wallace.

"Don't be jealous; I will teach you what I know."

Unbeknownst to him, Mr. Moss had just donated to the Minor Hill's Police Department and school system. Ava took custody of Mr. Moss and placed him in the back of her patrol car. Bixby was gracious enough to complete a background check and determined that Mr. Moss was a convicted felon.

"Mr. Moss, I will cut you a break on speeding fifteen miles over the speed limit. However, running the stop sign, possession of marijuana, firearm by a felon, and carrying a concealed weapon are non-negotiable. My hands are tied," Ava said softly sitting down in the driver's seat.

"Come on, I just started a new job. I have been trying to get on the right track ma'am."

"Hold onto my card. If you would like to provide me with a bigger fish, then you can work off these charges."

"I have kids to worry about. I can't be out here snitching. DAMN!"

"We can provide you with protection. Take some time to think about it. Car 2-4-6 I will be transporting one male to county."

"Copy," communications acknowledged.

Ava rolled down her window, "Thanks for the help Corporal."

"No, thank you Officer Singleton. You have changed my mind about women working in this profession. I learned that you can truly hold your own. Shit, you have the highest arrests, citations, warning tickets, and completed reports on the squad. I will be recommending you for Officer of the Month. Now take his ass to jail."

"Yes sir," Ava laughed. Truth be told, it was slightly rewarding hearing those words coming out his mouth.

The next day in line-up, Sgt. Fitzpatrick asked, "Who wants to take lead on this service complaint? Several anonymous crime stoppers tips have been received regarding an illegal liquor house."

Looking around the room Ava raised her hand, "I will Serge."

Ava wasted no time stepping into a leadership role and delegating tasks.

"Lynn, I need you to conduct stationary surveillance. Bixby and Stewart, I want you to stop vehicles leaving the residence. Be sure to give the vehicles some time to travel far enough from the residence to avoid drawing attention. Quinn and Jones if you all can position in areas to assist with the traffic stops when the call load allows, that will be great."

"Got it, but before we go out there…what do you guys think about me proposing to my girlfriend with a blood diamond?" Bixby asked distracted.

The squad laughed and exited the room. Bixby was in need of special prayer. Ava hoped the traffic stops would yield enough information so she could apply for a search warrant. To establish probable cause, Ava needed to show the intoxicated subjects were leaving the residence, and driving.

Lynn got out on foot and stood behind some trees at a meat packaging business. The location was perfect for Lynn to maintain a visual of the residence. Bixby and Stewart were positioned east and west of the residence; while Quinn and Jones positioned themselves north and south. Two weeks into the operation, the squad had several successful traffic stops and trash pulls consistent with the running of an illegal liquor house. With Sgt. Fitzpatrick's guidance, Ava applied for her first search warrant that was approved by the magistrate. Southwest Squad S successfully executed the search warrant with assistance from the Tactical Narcotics Team. Together, the squad totally dismantled the liquor house that was disrupting the quality of life for the residents.

Ava took the honor of pouring the many bottles of untaxed liquor down the drain. Meanwhile, Stewart had located a pound of weed, an eight ball of crack, and four bundles of heroin in the air vent. To top it off, Ava found a stolen assault rifle between a mattress and box spring. Ava could sense the neighbors' relief, watching the homeowner being placed in the back of the patrol car. News traveled fast that Southwest Squad S was the squad to emulate, due to their high standards, camaraderie, and hard work.

Ava's probationary period ended, allowing her to work supplemental assignments for additional compensation. The timing was perfect, being that JaQuan had just graduated at the top of his high school class. She would now be able to contribute more towards JaQuan's college expenses. Most of Ava's friends had younger brothers who were either incarcerated or having children out of wedlock. Thankfully her brother didn't fall into that same boat.

Ava worked every weekend during the sweltering summer. She provided additional security for a few night clubs and community events. The work wasn't hard, but standing on her feet for hours on end was a battle. Severe foot pain prompted Ava to visit a podiatrist who diagnosed her with plantar fasciitis and arthritis. Working through the pain, she managed to make an extra $5,250.00 that summer. Without a second thought, Ava gave the money to JaQuan to assist with his first year of college. That no-good Braxton wasn't going to help and she couldn't allow Agni to bear the burden alone. Even if she had to stand on one leg, Ava was determined her brother would have all the essential tools to be successful in college.

CHAPTER 6

USE OF FORCE

If there was such a thing as "verbal judo" then Ava would receive a black belt in the discipline. She had the natural ability to talk someone off a bridge and deescalate hostile situations. Ava had been working patrol for three years and still hadn't used force to control a non-compliant subject.

Lynn and Ava were dispatched to a domestic dispute in a subsidized housing apartment on a rainy afternoon. The call notes advised that a female was heard yelling, "Help! Stop hitting me!" The caller who wished to remain anonymous, advised emergency communications that it sounded like an active disorder was taking place. Ava caught a glimpse of a black female running across the parking lot when she arrived.

"Excuse me Ma'am. Can you please come talk to me?" Ava yelled out her window.

"Yeah, my dumb ass baby daddy at it again."

85

"What's your name?"

"Shatayia Miller," she replied holding a blood-soaked napkin against her nose. Her right eye was swollen and a portion of her weave was missing from the apparent struggle.

"Ms. Miller what is going on tonight? Do you want me to call EMS to check you out?"

"No, I'm fine. We started fighting because he sits around playing video games all day and don't help with our two kids." Ms. Miller brushed off her jeans that had fresh holes in them and wiped off her face with a blood drenched t-shirt.

Lynn arrived on scene taking primary to fulfill her zone duties, "What's his name?"

"B-Rich. He should be in your system. That nigga ain't bout shit."

"Where is he now Ms. Miller?"

"'He left with one of his homeboys."

"Okay. Do you mind if I have our Crime Scene Investigator take a couple of photos of your injuries?"

"Yes, I do mind. I'm not down with that."

By this point, Ava had enough and got on her soapbox hoping Lynn would keep a straight face.

"I am a twenty-three-year old single mother of two young boys myself. I was once in your shoes, unemployed and depending on a man for my every need. However, I decided enough is enough. I took some classes online and completed the Minor Hill's Police Academy. I know that you want to be something greater than a baby mama with a sorry baby daddy."

Ms. Miller looked Ava in the eye and begin to nod her head "yes."

Lynn starred at a hole in the apartment building trying to maintain her composure. She couldn't look at Ava without laughing, knowing that she was lying through her teeth. The closest thing Ava had to a child was a four-legged spoiled-rotten dog. Not ready to step off her soapbox, Ava continued.

"If he puts his hands on you once, he will do it again. What if he takes it too far? Your children lose their mother to the hands of their father and their father will be lost to the prison system. Do you want them to grow up thinking that a man's purpose is to degrade women? Ms. Miller, you are so much better than this."

"You right, Officer Singleton. I'm going to get my life together. I have no choice but to change for my kids." Ms. Miller began to break down crying.

"I believe you will Ms. Miller, and I will be praying for you. We are required to write a report about this incident. See the North Carolina law requires officers responding to domestic calls, to make an arrest if there are any signs of injury. To uphold my civic duty, I will be stopping by the magistrate's office to swear out a warrant on B-Rich for Assault on a Female." Ava spoke calmly to Ms. Miller.

"I understand you have a job to do."

"Last thing, please go by the magistrate's office and take out a 50B Restraining Order on B-Rich. We are doing our part, but you need to do yours. Be safe, Ms. Miller." Ava handed Ms. Miller her business card with her personal cell phone number.

Ava and Lynn met up at a dead-end street.

"Singleton, you're crazy girl. You got two kids my ass."

Ava smiled, "I made a connection with her and hopefully our heart-to-heart makes a difference in her life."

Lynn had taken a liking to Ava, she would always head in Ava's direction if she stopped a car, got dispatched alone, or wanted to self-initiate on any suspicious activity.

Despite the smile on her face, Ms. Miller had caused Ava to reminisce about her childhood. There was a time when eight-year old Ava witnessed Braxton's "bitch-ass" kicking her pregnant mother in the stomach. Ava pleaded with Agni to leave Braxton, but her mother feared the thought of raising another child without a father. Sadly, Agni subjected herself to the cycles of abuse; tension building, acute battering, and the honeymoon phase.

Once Agni told Ava, "You are just jealous because you don't have a father."

Those were the harshest words Ava ever heard come out of her mother's mouth. In the moment, Ava hid in her bedroom closet weeping. Unable to express herself, she began acting out in fourth grade and had to receive disciplinary action. The idea that Ava wanted her future siblings to grow up without a father was far from the truth. Later in life, Ava began to understand the perspective of an abused woman.

While an undergraduate, Ava was tasked to find a guest speaker for her Introductory Psychology course. After some thought, she decided that her mother would be the perfect candidate. Agni stood in front of the class, speaking on the cycles of domestic violence and how she once fell victim. She told a heroine's story of going from victim to victor. Watching Agni speak brought peace to Ava, knowing that she had the qualities of a remarkable woman built into her DNA.

After the presentation, Ava sat down with Agni at their favorite deli. Agni apologized for some of the hurtful things she said to Ava growing up and for exposing her to the toxic relationship with Braxton. Before Agni could cry, Ava gave her a hug.

"Ma, don't worry about any of that. I have let it go and forgiven you. Let's not dwell in the past, but let's look forward to the future. We have come a long way as a family." *Exodus 20:12, "Honour your father and your mother, that your days may be long upon the land which the Lord your God is giving you."*

See, police work was more than making arrests, doing searches, and catching bad guys. Unlike any other job in America, police officers wear multiple hats. Police officers work as advocates, psychologists, and protectors. In addition, they must be relatable, finding common ground with citizens to enhance the community they serve.

Ava and Lynn realized that society was changing. The male criminals used to respect lady officers based on their gender alone, but those were the days of the past. Lately, it seemed that the streets of Minor Hills wanted to give them a run for their money. The pair were given the nicknames "Ebony" and "Ivory" in the line-up room. The monikers were an ode to the 1982 number one single, "Ebony and Ivory" by Stevie Wonder and Paul McCartney. The hit song addressed racial inequality using the black and white piano keys as a metaphor. Ironically, Ava was called "Ebony" and Lynn was "Ivory."

Sunday morning on routine patrol, Ava observed the signature white work van driven by child molesters. The van sat through a green light with the driver's door open. Next, the van turned on its left turn signal, cut the steering wheel, and remained stationary. Ava's suspicion meter was rising watching the van sit through an additional light cycle. The van's tag light was inoperable and curiosity overwhelmed Ava.

"Car 2-4-6 I will be 10-38."

"Go ahead Car 2-4-6."

"Liberty St. at Green Tree Rd., out with North Carolina Registration Delta-Delta-Charlie-X-X-X-X. Will be on an older white van unknown make or model."

Ava got out of the car and slowly approached the driver who was identified as Matthew Ray. Mr. Ray was a white male, sallow skin, approximately thirty-three years of age, 5'8, and one hundred and sixty pounds. He had an absurd brown mullet and a blank stare. The hairs on the back of Ava's neck stood up when she shined her light on Mr. Ray. The man was completely covered in dirt from his head to his feet. Automatically assuming the worse, Ava thought he could have killed someone and disposed of the body in a makeshift grave.

"Why are you covered in dirt? It's 2 o' clock in the morning?" Ava asked while focusing on his hands.

"I've just been doing some construction work?"

"That's interesting because the city ordinance doesn't allow construction after 2100 hours. Do you have your license and registration sir?" Lynn walked up to the vehicle to check on Ava.

"Yes, ma'am I do," he replied nervously handing Ava his license and registration.

Ava whispered to Lynn. "Standby with him because something isn't right. He is covered in mud. I'm going to run his information and try to get a search on the van."

Surprisingly, the crossbred southern belle intertwined with an suburban upbringing had impeccable street smarts. Ava learned Mr. Ray had a prior criminal history that included larceny from a construction site. Armed with the new information, Ava shined her flashlight through the windows of the van. Stopping at the trunk's rear window, she noticed approximately fifty pounds of copper pipes covered in fresh mud.

"Mr. Ray, I need you to step out of the vehicle so we can talk about some things." Ava demanded.

"Okay," he said exiting the vehicle.

"What is all this copper doing in the back of the vehicle?"

"I was moving some pipes from the church."

"What church was that?"

"Yeah...I don't know the name of it. It's in the county."

"Mr. Ray please place your hands behind your back. You are being detained." Mr. Ray failed to comply and began to reach into his front left pocket.

"Sir! Stop Reaching!" Ava and Lynn yelled simultaneously.

Ava grabbed Mr. Ray's right arm that he was using to reach into his pocket. When Ava lifted his arm a glass pipe fell to the ground. Lynn attempted to gain control of his left arm.

"What you going to do to me?" Mr. Ray asked while actively resisting and trying to "man handle" the lady officers.

Ava keyed up on the radio, "Start us some cars!" She was aware Mr. Ray was in fight mode.

"Car 2-4-6, we have Cars 2-5-6 and 2-1-6 en-route emergency traffic." Communications dispatched Jones and Stewart to assist.

Ava was still holding on to Mr. Ray's right hand while Lynn was gaining control of his left hand. Mr. Ray attempted to elbow Lynn in the face, but Ava quickly sprang into action. She took him back to her soccer days and kicked his feet from underneath him. Mr. Ray face-planted on the hard concrete. As a result, he sustained a broken nose and a laceration to his forehead. Not on her watch was someone going to harm Lynn or any other officers she worked with.

"Help! The police whooping my ass!" Mr. Ray yelled.

Lynn gained full control of Mr. Ray's left arm and Ava handcuffed him. Unfortunately, he wasn't finished acting a fool. Mr. Ray began to kick the back-seat windows of the patrol vehicle at the same time Jones and Stewart arrived on scene. The guys of Southwest Squad S didn't take a liking to cowardly men disrespecting their lady counterparts. Jones and Stewart pulled Mr. Ray out of the patrol car and maximally restrained him with a rip hobble. The rip hobble was placed around Mr. Ray's legs to prevent him from hurting himself or others.

Jones told Mr. Ray, "There is no point for you to be kicking sir.

You already got your ass beat by two females." Ava and Lynn looked at each other and burst out laughing uncontrollably.

"Man, shut up," Mr. Ray muttered under his breath.

Mr. Ray was transported to the jail without further incident.

"Girl, we have to hit the weight room full force. The streets keep trying us," Ava stated while flexing her arm muscles.

"I know a free mixed martial arts course on Tuesday and Wednesday nights."

"Well you know free is definitely my language. Give me a time and I will be there, Ivory."

Ava reported to the line-up room as usual the next day, but one officer was missing. Sgt. Fitzpatrick, Cpl. Wallace, Quinn, Bixby, Stewart, and Lynn were all accounted for.

Sgt. Fitzpatrick began line-up, "Officer Jones has resigned from the department. If you see him later today, he is only here to turn in all his police equipment." The Southwest Squad S looked at Sgt. Fitzpatrick in dismay.

He continued perturbed, "I can't elaborate because there is an ongoing investigation regarding allegations against him in Internal Affairs. I'm going to go ahead and wrap this up. You all be safe tonight."

Ava whispered to Lynn while walking down the hallway, "Girl, you have to find out what's going on with Jones." See, Lynn's father had retired from the police department with both rank and respect. Ava knew that she could make a few phone calls to find out what was going on.

"Oh, I already got the tea. Meet me in the back of the parking lot after you load up your patrol car so I can spill it." Lynn replied shaking her hair to one side dramatically.

"Please spill the tea," Ava petitioned while partially hanging out of her patrol vehicle.

"Girl, I heard that Jones had two choices: resign and keep his law enforcement certification or wait on Internal Affairs and risk termination.

"Say what?" Ava asked.

"They say he responded to a domestic dispute with only one-party present. The party present was a middle-aged woman who had been nicknamed "Butter face." You know everything looked good on her, But-Her-Face." Lynn began choking off her own laughter.

"Girl stop lying," Ava chuckled.

"Okay, so good old Jones saw the damsel in distress and dipped his pen in company ink…possibly in the company car. Casually having sex with the woman while he was on duty being paid by the police department."

"No way!"

"Yes, apparently Internal Affairs has received anonymous video footage and photographic evidence to support the claim."

"Damn!" Ava yelled in disbelief. She couldn't believe Jones of all people would jeopardize his family and career.

That was the end of Jones who was never witnessed in Minor Hills again. The rumor mill alleged that he moved out west with his family and joined a federal agency. Southwest Squad S was down a man and would have to wait for the next police academy to graduate recruits.

Later that night, the dispatcher came over the radio: "Car 2-4-6, 2-5-6, 2-1-6 and 2-3-6 need you to respond to the Minor Hill's Inn, reference a naked man trying to break in a motel room through a glass window."

"Copy," all units responded.

While in police academy the recruits learned that any call involving a naked man would likely involve a use of force. Ava tried to develop a plan of action before arriving on the scene but that wasn't working out so well. Only dirty thoughts crossed her mind about the front seat tickets to the male strip show she was about to witness.

Quinn, Bixby, Stewart, and Ava arrived on scene at the same time. Ava and Quinn approached on foot from the west, while Bixby and Stewart approached from the east.

Ava told Quinn, "You can go hands on and I will be less than lethal." Turning on her Taser with the red beaming light activated.

"Why do you want me to go hands on with the naked man?" Quinn asked unsettled.

"You used to be the lightweight boxing champion. Plus, I don't know how much of an effect the windmill might have on this guy."

Ava and Quinn cut the corner tactfully and observed the naked man. The man had dark skin, approximately forty-two years of age, 5'5, severely obese, mini afro, untamed beard, and a FUPA. Ava had learned the term "FUPA" from Bixby one day in line up. Thankfully Bixby gave the code word "earmuffs" before explaining the acronym.

The word "FUPA" translated to Fat Upper Pubic Area. The naked man's belly fat was concealing his man business. The man's nickname on the street was "Big Daddy Black." Ava was confused because the nickname "Big Daddy Lack" seemed more fitting.

It was safe to say that Big Daddy Black was under the influence of an impairing substance. He was standing on shards of glass seemingly immune to the pain. The trash can he used to break the window was within arms-reach.

Ava began to give loud verbal commands, "Sir, drop the trash can! I need you to come over here so we can talk to you!"

"No. I can't right now! The bitch inside this room owes me sex. I took this hoe out for a steak dinner; she gonna give me some pussy!" Big Daddy Black yelled ignorantly. Out the corner of Ava's eye, she noted Bixby and Stewart closing in distance from the east.

"Sir, that is unfortunate. Come on over here so we can talk about it. I see that you are bleeding and I want to get you some help," Ava attempted to reason.

Big Daddy Black kicked the trash can over and grabbed a piece of shard glass approximately four inches long. The officers began stepping back for their safety.

"Drop it or I'm going to tase you!" Ava yelled while placing the red beaming light on his FUPA. Big Daddy Black had a death stare in his eyes and refused to comply. Suddenly he began to charge at the officers.

Ava slowly pulled the trigger yelling, "Taser...Taser...Taser!"

Both Taser probes made contact with his stomach and had a five-inch spread. Big Daddy Black began to shake, the glass shard fell out of his hand, and muddy water started running down the back of his leg. Bixby and Stewart placed handcuffs on him.

"I need a supervisor to respond reference use of force and EMS for probe removal." Ava advised police communications.

Sgt. Fitzpatrick arrived on scene, "What happened?"

"Serge, shit happened, literally," Ava replied in shock. She had just popped her taser cherry.

"What am I going to do with you Singleton?" Sgt. Fitzpatrick shook his head and laughed inwardly.

After EMS removed the probes and cleaned Big Daddy Black up, Ava and Quinn transported him down to county. He was charged with attempted Breaking and Entering, Resisting a Public Officer, and Vandalism. The magistrate held him under no bond due to pending charges.

CHAPTER 7

HANDS UP, DON'T SHOOT

At approximately 0240 hours, Cpl. Wallace keyed up on the radio.

"I am trying to catch up to a vehicle driving at an extremely high rate of speed. We are traveling southbound on Interstate 23 passing the Franklin St. exit."

"Copy. Can you advise what type of car?"

"No! The vehicle is traveling over 100 mph. Be advised vehicle almost struck a motorcycle, in pursuit."

"Car 2-4-6 start that way. I will be pulling two other cars from a different district as they are showing to be closer."

"Copy," Ava responded.

Ava had been sitting in her patrol vehicle to deter criminals from stealing catalytic converters. She was all too eager to join the action, quickly activating her emergency lights and sirens. Ava jumped on Interstate 23 desperately trying to catch up.

"Cpl. I'm right behind you, as well as three other cars ready to perform a mobile roadblock on your count." She finally saw his blue lights after driving over 100 mph for a grueling five minutes. Thankfully there was little to no traffic out, since Ava was pushing the Ford Crown Victoria to its extremes.

"Copy. Move on three," Cpl. Wallace advised.

Cpl. Wallace pulled in front of the vehicle at an angle forcing Ava to stop directly behind the suspect vehicle. While exiting her patrol car, Ava observed a black male with a bald head exiting the suspect vehicle. The man dropped a black object and took off running.

"Let me see your hands! Stop running!" Ava yelled unsure if the suspect dropped a gun or a phone. She instantly broadcasted an alert to the dispatcher and took off running with her gun in tow.

The subject had a head start and the advantage of not wearing a police-issued duty belt. Ava was determined to keep up and continued running. Cpl. Wallace and the other assist officers weren't too far behind, but Ava was leading the pack. She chased the subject, later identified as Casey Potts, for a quarter of a mile. Periodically flashing her strobe light on Mr. Potts to throw him off balance. Suddenly he became fatigued, vomited, and dropped down to his knees with his hands up.

Ava immediately placed handcuffs on Mr. Potts for the numerous driving infractions and resisting a public officer. A check with police communications determined that he had a nonextraditable probation violation out of Georgia.

"Thanks for having my back Singleton. Do you mind taking him down to the jail so I can start on the paperwork?" Cpl. Wallace asked, clearly flustered.

"Not at all; it would be my pleasure." Ava began walking Mr. Potts to her patrol vehicle.

"Wait! Officers, I'm so sorry. I was just trying to get home so I could take my daughter to church in the morning. Don't know what cops will do these days. Is there anything I can do to get out this mess?" Mr. Potts asked in a remorseful tone.

"Are you serious? You want a break after a vehicle and foot pursuit? Don't you know that cell phone you dropped, could have easily been mistaken for a handgun? You were almost another statistic tonight. Do you hear what I'm saying?" Ava vociferated.

"Yes, ma'am," Mr. Potts replied nodding his head.

"Police officers have to make sure they make it back home to their families too. You made some dumb mistakes tonight. I want you to promise that you are going to do better. Not for me but for your daughter, Mr. Potts."

"I promise I will, ma'am. Do you think there is any way I could get a citation? I really need to pick up my daughter and attend church in the morning."

"Look, you need to talk to Cpl. Wallace because the decision lies with him."

"Cpl. Wallace, is there any way you can help me sir? I promised my little girl. I'm such an idiot." Mr. Potts begged.

"What church do you attend Mr. Potts?"

"Mt. Zion Baptist Church, sir."

"Okay what time do we all need to be at church?" Cpl. Wallace asked looking at his watch.

"11 o'clock sir."

"Well since I'm towing your car, I will be at your house at 10:30 in the morning for church. I'll even give you a ride home."

"Yes sir, thank you. Be ready to hear some good music, Corporal."

"I might see yawl there. That's my Grandma's church." Ava chimed in.

Bixby who unofficially assigned himself to the vehicle pursuit walked up to Ava. "Damn, Singleton. I didn't know you had some jets on you. You were moving fast as hell."

"Well you are looking at the former Minor Hills High School Athlete of the Year." Ava joked arrogantly.

Distracted, Bixby asked, "Is our Cpl. getting soft? I swear he is acting like his balls haven't dropped. He just gave that man the break of a lifetime." Ava could only shake her head.

A few hours later, Ava accompanied Grandma Rose to Mt. Zion Baptist Church.

The church elder finished reading the announcements and asked, "Do we have any new visitors here today?" Ava remained seated believing she was in the clear; throughout the years she had visited the church, so she wasn't technically a "new visitor."

The church elder took off her church hat to look at the congregation. "I'm not like some of our other greeters. I know I see some unfamiliar faces. Please introduce yourself if you haven't been here in a while." Ava could feel Grandma Rose giving her a side eye.

She stood up, "My name is Ava Singleton and it's a pleasure to fellowship with you today, saints. I am currently a member of Minor Hills Baptist Church. My father was the late Reverend Singleton. I didn't stand up the first time because I feel like this is my church home away from home. Thank you."

The congregation appeared overjoyed at seeing the late Reverend Singleton's daughter all grown up. A few more visitors introduced themselves. Cpl. Wallace, Mr. Potts, and his 5-year-old daughter haphazardly entered the church while the church elder went on a tangent.

"I have something else I need to tell you church. One of our young black boys sitting in the choir today was at the church last night. Somehow he accidently set off the alarm and the police responded. The officer asked him, "What are you doing on the church grounds on a Saturday night, boy? Do you have any identification?" Our young black boy told the officer, "I'm just cleaning up sir, and here is my identification." Our young black boy could have been one of the many unarmed black men losing their life to the hands of the police. All I want to say is, "Hands up, Don't Shoot!" The church elder yelled while standing at the podium.

The pianist struck a chord on the keys and the choir stood up and chanted, "Hands up, Don't Shoot!"

Ava's mouth nearly touched the floor watching the choir. Mr. Potts and the young black boy in the choir both had an encounter with the police in less than twenty-four hours. Although the contact was warranted, any contact with police involving blacks was often misconstrued and labeled as racism. Pretending to stretch, Ava looked behind to gage Cpl. Wallace's expression. He was the only white man in a predominantly black church. From Ava's vantage point he appeared to blend in just fine with his three-piece pin stripped suit.

Historically, the church had been a meeting place for organizing non-violent protest during the Civil Rights movement. The house of the Lord doubled as a safe-haven that aimed to annihilate racial discrimination, segregation, and inequality. Ava sat in dismay trying to comprehend the churches antics. Growing up a pastor's daughter, Ava knew that the church was supposed to represent the body of Christ. *1 Corinthian 12:12, "For as the body is one and has many members, but all the members of that one body, being many, are one body: so also is Christ."*

The saying, "Hands Up, Don't Shoot" started when an unarmed black man was killed in an urban area by a white male police officer. Ava watched the deceased teenager become the poster child for mistrust between the black community and law enforcement. Several witnesses present during the shooting reported that the teenager's hands were up in the air, surrendering peacefully to the police officer. However, others said the young man did not have his hands up and portrayed him as a hardened criminal who used illegal drugs. Ava learned through police gossip the main witness of this highly publicized shooting was later found murdered. The story of unarmed black men being killed at the hands of white police officers was one that Ava knew well. Personally, she believed the tragedies correlated to inadequate training and lack of education.

Every week she witnessed news media outlets making it their mission to broadcast the killing of unarmed black men at the hands of white male police officers. America was outraged and violent protest erupted throughout the nation. Looters were Christmas shopping, stealing everything from flat screen televisions to forty-ounce beers. Angry protesters were burning down churches, police vehicles, and fast food restaurants. Ava watched major cities enter a state of national emergency due to the civil unrest.

As the pastor walked to the pulpit, the congregation stood to their feet. "Thank you, please be seated. Now, I'm glad the officer investigated because someone could have been breaking into our church," the pastor giggled uncomfortably. Ava was relieved that someone in the house of the Lord was open-minded.

"Church, can I keep it real for a minute?" The pastor asked sipping on a glass of water.

"Yes! Preach, Preacher!" Members of the congregation shouted.

"Well I'm going to take it there this morning. I want you to know that we can't expect our young people to surrender to the police when they haven't surrendered to Christ. Church, can you hear me? I know that some people in here today are just blindly going through the motions of living life. Not knowing they are only existing. Church, I want you to know that you can only truly live when you give your life to Christ. Please turn to *Galatians 2:20*. When you find it say, "Amen.""

"Amen," the churchgoers replied unanimously.

"Let's read this verse together," the pastor instructed.

Galatians 2:20, "I have been crucified with Christ; it is no longer I who live, but Christ lives in me; and the life which I now live which I now in the flesh I live by faith in the Son of God, who loved me and gave himself for me." The church read in unison.

The pastor continued, "We can chant, "Hands Up, Don't Shoot" in protest with our hands in the air, but I want to declare unto you today, that if we don't put our hands up for the Lord...Jehovah-Jireh, The King of Kings, God Almighty then Church, our young people are going to continue to fail to surrender. See *Isaiah 40:28-31 says, "Have you not known? Have you not heard? The everlasting God, the Lord, the Creator of the ends of the earth, Neither faints nor is weary? His understanding is unsearchable. He gives power to the weak, And to those who have no might He increases strength. Even the youths shall faint and be weary, And the young men shall utterly fall, But those who wait on the Lord Shall renew their strength; They shall mount up with wings like eagles; They shall run and not be weary; They shall walk and not faint."* See what I came to say Church… is that we need to surrender ourselves to Christ. We can't keep just existing; it's time we start living. I know that it is trying times, but the time has come... The time is now to start living for the Lord."

"Yes Lord," Ava stated standing up inspired by the sermon.

The drummer began striking the drums in rapid succession. Naturally the entire church began to clap their hands and stomp their feet. A young boy was playing his tambourine at a high frequency. The church band appeared to be possessed with the spirit of legends from the last century. A fusion of negro spirituals, jazz, bluegrass, and modern trap gospel sounded throughout the church. The Holy Ghost power was in Mt. Zion Hill Baptist Church. A few people began shouting while others took a victory lap around the church.

Unbeknownst to Ava, Cpl. Wallace had been secretly battling his own personal demons. For years, Cpl. Wallace had been burdened with guilt, after losing his daughter tragically. Cpl. Wallace was plagued by memories of the dreadful day when he was monitoring prostitutes online, instead of his young daughter who laid unresponsive at the bottom of their swimming pool.

"Is there anyone here today who's ready to give their life to Christ? Please come forward with an open heart." The pastor invited.

The Holy Ghost power was moving like the wind touching every soul in the pews. It was almost as if the spirit of the Lord was guiding the steps of the young boy who set off the church alarm. He slowly rose out of his seat and walked to the alter with his hands raised surrendering to GOD. A few more young people followed suit, trickling down to the alter.

Cpl. Wallace began having vivid flashbacks of his daughter's last moments. Clarity engulfed him. He began making his way down to the alter, guided to the path of righteousness by a familiar young angel. A glimmer of hope traveled through Ava walking down to support her brother in law enforcement.

The pastor placed his anointed hands on Cpl. Wallace who dropped down to his knees "Yes, Lord continue to touch his spirit and renew this man."

Seized by the love of God, Cpl. Wallace finally forgave himself for his daughter's death. *Philippians 4:7, "And the peace of God, which surpasses all understanding, will guard your hearts and minds through Christ Jesus."*

The whole congregation stood to their feet as the pastor concluded with the benediction prayer.

"Our Father,"

The congregation joining in, "Who art in heaven, hallowed be thy name..."

CHAPTER 8

TWELVE

Back at work, Ava understood she was living in a society that lacked obedience to God. Ava didn't expect mankind to obey the laws of the land because mankind wouldn't even obey God. Looking at the bright side, Ava saw job security in a less than favorable police climate. Of course, a small part of the population loved police and believed they could do no wrong. There were a few neutral law-abiding citizens who were indifferent to the propaganda. However, there was an increasing population that hated police altogether.

Ava became accustomed to the name-calling that came with wearing a police uniform. The words "12," "5-0," "Pig," "Ops," and "Po-Po" were extremely popular. Members of the Minor Hills community would use the slang to warn local drug dealers that police were in the area, pass interference on other criminal activities, and just express hatred towards the police. Rap songs were filled with lyrics detailing the lack of trust and mistreatment by the hands of the police. For some, rap culture was more influential than religion. Many believed there was no difference between unarmed black men of today being shot to death by the police versus black men of yesteryears being lynched.

Injustice would not be swept under the rug on Ava's watch. She was determined to uphold the laws and serve her community. No way would she ever become a "dirty cop" selling-out her convictions for the amenities of being a police woman. Outside her uniform and badge, Ava was first a Christian woman who strived to do right in a world where the devil was very active.

"Car 2-4-6 and 2-5-6, I need you to respond to 134 Grove St. in reference to an active disorder." Both units copied.

"Be advised twenty-four-year old Jessica Baldwin is extremely intoxicated. Her father fears that she is a danger to herself. She has tried to walk out into the street but keeps falling down. The father is sitting on top of Ms. Baldwin and now has her in a choke hold."

"Copy. Show both units in the area," Ava advised communications.

Ava and Lynn got out of the car and observed Ms. Baldwin in a choke hold. Ava gave verbal commands to the father, "Sir, get off your daughter!"

Mr. Baldwin complied, "Misses Officer, I'm so sorry. Jessica has been acting a fool since she has been off her medication. She comes home drunk every night raising hell. She got a DWI last night and I'm tired of her. I don't want her to run out in the street and get hit by a car."

Jessica was a white female, shoulder length dark brown hair, green eyes, approximately 5'5, two hundred and fifteen pounds, with a mild case of acne. She was wearing a strapless dress that was two sizes too small. Furthermore, she had multiple tattoos and excessive piercings that didn't need to be on display.

"I hate you and your new little ass wife! Tell that hoe to eat a dick and die!" Jessica yelled at her father. Unable to focus, she directed her anger towards Ava.

"What are you doing, girl? You are black, don't you watch the news. Don't you know the police are killing your people? I mean really, what are you doing wearing that badge?"

Ava ignored Jessica's statements, raised to never answer to any name outside of her own. Ava was furious. In her mind, she cussed Jessica out and called her everything under the sun including a "female dog." Practicing patience and remaining professional in an atmosphere full of ignorance was a struggle for Ava.

Ava took a deep breath, "Ma'am, can you please go in the house and sleep off the alcohol?"

"No bitch, I'm walking away because I have rights," Jessica replied. Ava clinched her teeth and balled her fists.

Lynn attempted to reason with her, "I need you to go in the house so we don't have to take you to jail." Jessica stumbled to the ground.

Continuing to run her mouth, "Who is going to make me? I know you not, toothpick. Matter of fact, I will dunk both you Oreo Cookie Cop bitches with this whole milk." Ava had reached her ignorance limit for the day. She quickly moved in and placed handcuffs on

Jessica who was sitting upright on her knees.

No way was privileged Jessica getting a get out of jail free pass. She may have talked to her daddy any kind of way without consequences and repercussions, but not Officer Singleton. Jessica was held at the county jail overnight on an Intoxicated Subject Hold.

Leaving the sally port Ava was immediately dispatched, "Car 2-4-6."

"Go ahead," Ava replied.

"I need you to respond to 755 Gramble St. reference child endangerment. Anonymous caller advised three small children are constantly left unattended and is concerned for their safety."

"Copy." Ava acknowledged, familiar with the trailer park.

Upon her arrival, she observed a couple of broken down cars in the driveway. The house had trash bags covering the windows and trash itself masking the porch. Ava went to the front door and knocked. Light footsteps were heard inside of the residence, but no one came to the door. Peering into the window, she saw a little boy peeling back the makeshift blinds to peek outside. He locked eyes with Ava before covering the window back. Ava heard additional footsteps inside of the house and knocked again on the door.

With no answer at the door, Ava checked water resources. She determined Tierra Cook made a payment three days prior. Lynn stopped by and attempted to give Ms. Cook a call, but there was no answer. Since the caller wanted to remain anonymous it was impossible to ask follow-up questions. Ava began to grow weary. Any home with trash bags as window treatments was not a good sign.

Ava observed headlights beaming on the house. It was none other than Ms. Cook parking in the gravel driveway. She quickly jumped out of her raggedy car, slammed the driver's side door, and began ranting.

"What the hell is going on? Why the police at my mother fucking house? Are my kids okay? I get off work and come home to some bullshit!" An animated Ms. Cook spoke loudly as her oversized bubble gum machine fake gold hoop earrings, dangled with every neck-roll.

"Ma'am we are here to check on the well-being of your children. We received an anonymous call that they are constantly left unattended without adult supervision," Ava replied sternly.

"No, the hell they not. My brother is inside watching them right now."

"Ms. Cook we need to see the kids and verify they are not in danger." Ignoring Ava, Ms. Cook began searching for her house key and banging on the door.

Ms. Cook was becoming irate, "Trell, boy...you better open the damn door!" The same little boy peeled back the trash bag from the window to peek outside.

"Ma, I didn't open the door for the police." Trell uttered, opening the door with fear in his eyes. Ava immediately smelled the strong odor of burned marijuana emanating from inside the residence.

"Where in the hell is your uncle?"

"I don't know," Trell mumbled.

"Wait a minute! Who told you to come in my mother fucking house?!" Ms. Cook asked walking towards Ava and Lynn in an aggressive manner.

"Ma'am, we need to ensure that all of the children are safe inside of this house. Right now you are interfering with the investigation. Just so you're clear, we are not leaving until I have done so. Oh, and while I'm in this house, I run the show." Ava replied holding her ground stepping towards Ms. Cook.

"No, I think you need a search warrant." Ms. Cook bucked up ready to fight.

Ava understood constitutional law and knew that the strong odor of marijuana emanating from the residence equaled probable cause to detain Ms. Cook. Furthermore, the welfare of the children who had been left unattended created exigent circumstances. Authoritatively, Ava placed Ms. Cook in handcuffs to conduct a safety sweep of the residence.

"Ms. Cook, you are not under arrest. We just need to ensure the children are not in imminent danger." Ava announced, regretting the fact Trell had to witness his mom being placed in handcuffs. However, officer safety always took precedence. Both Ava and Lynn had families who anticipated their safe return home each day they walked out the front door.

Lynn stood by with Ms. Cook while Ava began to walk down a narrow hallway. There was a bathroom to her right that looked like it hadn't been cleaned in months. The toilet and tub had a black ring around the inside. Clothes were all over the floor. Proceeding down the hallway, Ava observed a bedroom to her left. Two young girls were sleeping peacefully on the floor accompanied by a few bed bugs. It did not appear to Ava that the girls were in any immediate danger. In the corner of the room Ava observed a dead mouse caught in the trap. Cognizant of her surroundings Ava began to take larger steps to cover more space. She learned in Biology that mice travel in social groups and knew more critters were likely running around the house. A five-year old boy had no business being responsible for his two younger sisters. Not to mention being responsible for himself. What if he was babysitting and there was an emergency? From the outside looking in, it didn't appear that Ms. Cook was the type to teach Trell to call 9-1-1 in the event of an emergency.

A second bedroom that lacked a bed was to the right. The room must have been Trell's, since small race cars and boy's clothes were all over the floor. At the end of the hall was a master bedroom equipped with a dirty mattress on the floor. In the kitchen, a combination of unwashed dishes and roaches were covering the countertop space. A blunt, grinder, and a $2.00 pack of hot fries were sitting on the table. Ava's skin began to itch, disgusted by the filth. She did not want to take any roaches home. Ms. Cook's children were being raised to disrespect authority figures and be nasty by their own mother. *Proverbs 22:6, "Train up a child in the way he should go, and when he is old he will not depart from it."*

Ava told Ms. Cook, "I'm going to treat you like a respectable young woman and mother by taking these handcuffs off you. However, you are going to have to calm down. Officer Lynn and I are here to help you and are only doing our jobs." Ms. Cook nodded her head and sat down on the couch.

"I am not going to speculate, but this is not my first rodeo. I don't know if the blunt is yours or your brothers. I do know that it has no reason being present in a household of small kids walking around unattended. This stops today, and I will be back to check on these children. I want you to understand that we could have easily taken you to jail and separated you from your children tonight. However, that is not what we are here for." Ava guided Ms. Cook to the bathroom and had her flush the blunt down the toilet. A lot of people smoke weed to ease the pain of life's stresses. A single blunt indicated the marijuana was for personal usage. Ava knew writing a citation for simple possession of marijuana wasn't going to benefit anybody involved in this situation.

On the flipside, if Ms. Cook would have had pounds of weed, digital scales, and clear plastic baggies the outcome would have been very different. Ava had witnessed too many people robbed, shot, and killed over drug deals gone wrong. No way would she cut Ms. Cook a break if she was a drug dealer. The risk of her house getting shot up and a bullet killing one of her kids was not going to be weighing on Ava's conscience. She understood the struggle of raising three small children as a single parent, working a minimum wage job in America.

Ava thought of her own mother, Agni when she looked at Ms. Cook. Agni had to hold down the fort, take care of three children, and deal with "fuckboy" Braxton's unemployed ass. Sometimes, Agni's credit card would get declined while she was trying to pay for groceries. Thankfully back in the day, there was always someone willing to share their food stamp wealth to expedite Agni from holding up the checkout line.

Ava informed Ms. Cook about the Child Response Program and the opportunities that it may provide her family. The program sponsored by Minor Hills Agricultural and Technical State University, helped children from the age of zero to eighteen who had suffered traumatic experiences, witnessed violence, or needed additional resources while living in underdeveloped communities. Over-achieving Ava had won the Southwest District Officer of the Year for making the most referrals to the program. Ms. Cook thanked Ava and shook her hand, but Ava wasn't quite ready to get off her soapbox yet.

"On another note, you are going to have to get this place cleaned up. I will give you some time, but I would be doing a disservice to your children if I didn't have the Department of Social Services follow-up."

"Okay. That's fair," Ms. Cook replied overcoming shame. The blind could see she never received a break from a police officer before. Ms. Cook had instantly judged Ava but soon realized she only had her children's best interest at heart.

Later, Ava looked at her computer screen and noticed several officers were on a traffic hazard call at 1344 Minor Hills Gardens. The area was notorious for gang activity. Call notes advised hundreds of people were outside walking in the street.

Ava added herself to the call and was brought up to speed by

Officer Quinn.

"So, check this, Singleton. A young black man was shot and killed at his baby mama's house while holding his two-year old daughter.

"Was the baby okay?" Ava asked devastated.

"Yeah, it's a blessing the bullet only grazed her leg. The streets are saying that the baby mama is partially responsible for the execution."

"Why would they say that?"

"She was trying to sell bootleg luxury purses to some customers. One of the customers was riding around with rival gang members who had beef with her baby daddy. While showing off the purses, gunfire suddenly erupted after a short verbal exchange."

"Man, this is awful. Who is willing to kill a man holding his daughter?"

Quinn looked down, "Our people."

The crowd had come together for the victim's vigil which was being broadcasted live on social media outlets. Ava could tell the crowd was experiencing a mix of emotions. The victim's homeboys were practicing the modern version of libation by pouring out their guzzling "40s." Family members were raising hell over the limited parking. Knowing this type of scenario all too well, commanding officers feared retaliation was inevitable. A few of the younger officers lacked sympathy, immediately trying to tow cars and kick people out of the street.

Luckily, quick-thinking Quinn had smoothed things over with the victim's family. The victim's brother had unknowingly caused the crowd after posting details of the vigil on public social media platforms. They were not expecting a massive crowd due to the short notice. A collage of the victim's photographs covered the front door of the aunt's house. A few candles were seen burning sporadically throughout the crowd. The sight was overwhelming for Ava who had never attended a vigil before.

"Where are the young men wearing suits?" Quinn asked.

Ava starred into the crowd and didn't see any young men in suits. The men were mostly wearing t-shirts, fitted caps, skinny jeans below their waist, and $200.00 tennis shoes. The women in the crowd weren't dressed appropriately either. They could have easily been mistaken as "working girls," flaunting what their mama gave them in a tasteless manner. Meanwhile, small children were running around unattended.

Towards the end of the vigil, a grown man looked Ava dead in her eyes and yelled, "Fuck 12!" Of course, he made the comment while sitting in the back seat of someone's car.

Ava felt disrespected, but couldn't expect more from a man who obviously lacked obedience to God. He was nothing more than a street punk likely raised by the streets. A real man would not curse at a female and then ride off. A real man would respect and love a Beautiful Black Queen. Speaking of such, Ava's love life was still a loss cause. She was actively dating a small basketball team of rejects. There was Mr. I Don't Have a Ride, Mr. I Am Looking for A Job but I'm an Actor, Mr. I'm Not That Confident to Date a Lady Cop in Public, Mr. I Make Six Figures so Bow Down to Me, and Mr. Call Me in the Middle of the Night.

If things weren't bad enough, Ava got dispatched to assist with a suspicious female flagging down cars on Martin Luther King Jr. Dr. A young officer who had just been released on solo assignment was dispatched to assist. En-route, Ava knew that the probability that it was an actual female was slim to none. The area was notorious for drugs and prostitution.

She arrived on scene and observed Bella walking in the middle of the street. Bella was dark skinned, approximately 6'3, one hundred and forty pounds, with a slim build. She was wearing a bad lace front wig, a dirty tank top, pencil skirt, and six-inch heels. Ava noticed Bella's Adam's apple sticking out like a sore thumb. However, at night there could be confusion. Ava had previously been introduced to Bella in field training.

"Bella, get out the street!"

"Yasss honey, I was just trying to make some money." Bella began walking towards Ava, twisting.

"Got a call saying you were flagging down cars."

"Well I can't lie to you, Officer Singleton."

"Bella, do you have anything illegal on you?"

"No, but let him search me." Bella smiled seductively at the rookie officer.

"Mind if I search your purse?" Ava asked.

"No, go ahead." Bella replied carelessly.

Inside the purse, Ava noticed a white pill and several condoms.

"What is this pill for?"

Bella quickly blurted, "Weight loss." Ava walked to the front of her patrol car to test the drugs. The rookie officer stood by with Bella and was later accompanied by Stewart.

"Ava, you're about to be pissed," Stewart whispered. Confused, Ava followed him back to where Bella and the rookie officer were standing.

"I didn't know *it* could do that. *It* just whipped it out so fast." The rookie stated in disbelief. Ava noticed a wet spot on the trunk of her Ford Crown Victoria and a trail of a wet fluid spreading on the ground.

"I know you didn't let Bella piss on my car, rookie!" Stewart began to laugh so hard he choked.

"We will talk later!" Ava cuffed up Bella and served *her* a first-class ticket to jail.

Ava couldn't believe the rookie allowed a transgender prostitute to piss on her patrol vehicle. That was the ultimate sign of disrespect. There was no telling what new diseases were floating around. Ava demanded the rookie clean her vehicle inside out that night.

The criminals of Minor Hills were getting bolder and bolder. Local thugs were walking around toting bigger guns than the police. The criminals knew that a lot of police officers were apprehensive to do their job. Thus, they assumed this greenlight as an opportunity to bring more guns and drugs onto the streets.

Social groups were coming together with the belief they had to police the police. Ava welcomed the public's idea of policing the police. She believed if everyday citizens would do a ride along for a day, they would have a different perspective of law enforcement. This would afford everyday citizens an opportunity to see firsthand the life of a police officer, in a society where they are constantly blamed for the tensions in America. Hearing the cries of the members of the public, the Minor Hills Police Department came up with a solution that utilized the advancement of technology. Soon a virtual babysitter would be monitoring police officers, making sure they were doing their job effectively.

CHAPTER 9

ROBOCOPS

That November Sgt. Fitzpatrick came into the squad line up room and announced, "With tensions between police and community rising, the Minor Hills Police Department has decided to move forward with equipping all uniformed officers with body worn cameras. I sent a departmental email that requires you to register for the Mandatory Body Worn Camera Training. Feel free to voice your opinion."

Stewart raised his hand, "Sir, I don't like the way it was presented to the department. I just feel like it's a way for officers to be monitored on a constant basis and eventually get hemmed up. I believe that it should have been presented in a way that makes us feel like the cameras are protecting us, the ones protecting and serving the community of Minor Hills. We risk our lives for nearly minimum wage, waiting for the big "IT" to happen, just to be persecuted by the media."

"Unfortunately, this is the new direction of policing. If you have an issue wearing the camera, I would highly recommend you look for a job somewhere else," Sgt. Fitzpatrick replied silencing the room.

After a small pause he continued passionately, "It is honestly only a matter of time before all police departments start equipping their officers with body worn cameras. We are going to have to change the way we police because everything is going to be scrutinized. Although we will be walking around looking like the 1987 film, *Robocop*, our job does not change. The camera initiative has gained massive appeal and support from the public. Due to recent events across the nation, cameras will protect the citizens as well as police officers. Personally, I'm glad that we are getting cameras because I know that we have a department full of great officers. I would like the Minor Hills Community to have the opportunity to see the same."

Ava sat at the table ingesting everyone's point of view and facial expressions. As far as she was concerned, there was no need for any further conversation on the matter. Sgt. Fitzpatrick had painted the picture perfectly; stay on the ship or drown. Ava was more concerned about how she would use the restroom with a police camera attached to her. Could the camera record her every move? What if it was a slow night at work and she wanted to talk to the latest guy friend from the online dating website "Pick-a-Fish No Catfish?" What about her right to privacy? On the other hand, Ava agreed with the president endorsing body worn cameras. Including the belief that every police department should utilize them. The cameras couldn't lie and would present the whole story, unlike the media.

A week later, Ava attended mandatory training for the body worn cameras taught by Sergeant Daniels. Sgt. Daniels was unfortunately given the task of researching various cameras to determine which product was the best fit for the Minor Hills Police Department and creating departmental policies that mandated officers to record certain calls. Everyone knew Sgt. Daniels would be getting promoted to Lieutenant soon for his dedication. It's nothing more than just police politics. Ava didn't know too much about Sgt. Daniels, other than his close friendship with Leduc. Later, she heard that Sgt. Daniels shot and killed someone while on duty. Ava noticed a sticker on his notebook that read, "Guns don't kill people. Men with mustaches do."

During training, Sgt. Daniels explained why he selected the camera with the durable design, thirty second buffer, mobile application, auto activation, and the ability to adjust to low light conditions. Everyone in the training class had to select two mounts to affix their body worn camera. The choices were a headset, polarized sunglasses, a baseball cap, or a shoulder piece. Ava selected the headset and sunglasses since she was a little shorter than the average person. The two mounts selected would hold Ava's camera at eye level; thus, if anything she did was ever questioned, the camera would present everything she was seeing at the time and record the full incident.

In a simplistic fashion, Sgt. Daniels broke down the use of the body worn camera, letting the class follow along with a hands-on approach.

Bixby was the first to ask a question, "So if I take a leak thirty seconds before stopping a car or getting to a call, are my family jewels going to be on camera?"

"Depends on the placement of your camera. If your camera was facing down in that direction, then yes. Don't be surprised if we have a police database full of dicks floating on some storage cloud," Sgt. Daniels replied. The class chuckled, reminiscent of a middle school sex education course. Ava's mind went off into the gutter thinking that a police database full of dicks wouldn't necessarily be a bad thing.

Sgt. Daniels advised the videos would have to be labeled and uploaded using a smart phone or computer before an officer ended their shift. Also, another caveat to the cameras was that if an officer attempted to record or screenshot the video footage, an email would automatically be sent to internal affairs. In turn, the officer could be subject to an internal investigation and face termination depending on the findings. Training was over just in time. Ava needed a moment to digest the new changes. It was a hard pill to swallow, knowing her badge that once represented honesty was no more. In hindsight, Ava would ultimately sacrifice her right to privacy for the greater good of the people. Even if it took her walking around with an electronic babysitter.

The Chief hosted a Question and Answer Session at the Community Center regarding the body worn cameras. The event was broadcasted on the local 6 o'clock news later that evening.

"Thank you all for coming out. The Minor Hill's Police

Department is moving forward with the body worn cameras to build trust between the community and police. I will take a couple of questions now," The Chief advised, stepping to the podium.

"Thank you Chief. I'm glad my caveman husband retired from law enforcement ten years ago. I don't think he would be able to keep up with all this new technology. How are the officers liking the cameras? An upbeat senior aged woman asked.

"The majority of the officers at Minor Hills are enthusiastic about the Body Worn Cameras because it can protect them from false allegations of misconduct. They will be primarily worn for accountability and evidence collection."

A middle-aged black lady asked, "So how long before the videos are altered? We see on the news how dirty these cops are." Her tone made it clear that all her sons were incarcerated.

The Chief responded, "No, the footage can't be altered or erased. The point of the body worn cameras is that they can't be manipulated or edited. Supervisors will be conducting checks on their officers' video footage to ensure the citizens are being treated with the utmost respect."

"How invasive will the cameras be regarding a citizen's right to privacy?" A college student inquired.

"The body worn cameras are new to law enforcement. Our constitutional laws were written in a time where technology barely existed. Our police attorney is researching privacy concerns and legalities. However, the courts have said that an individual doesn't have an expectation to privacy in a public setting. Also, it does appear that if an officer has the legal right to be somewhere, they have the right to record."

"What policies does the department have in place for the body cameras?" A famed local news reporter asked after applying a fresh layer of make-up.

"Currently, whenever one of our officers responds to a domestic dispute, effects an arrest, is involved in a vehicle pursuit, has a use of force, conducts a traffic stop, or has a consensual encounter involving criminal activity their camera will be activated. I have time for one more question." The Chief advised, staring at the wall clock.

"How will I know when I'm being recorded on an officer's body worn camera?" A clueless man asked scratching his head.

"If you are having a conversation with an officer, it is safe to assume that you are being recorded. Our officers will abide by the departmental policies and will be properly trained. I would like to thank everyone for coming out tonight, but we will be ending it here." The Chief walked away from the podium, shaking a few hands before exiting the community center.

Southwest Squad S took to the streets with their new Body Worn Cameras. Ava walked into the old gas station, with her camera attached to her headset mount. Detail was in the parking lot when he observed the camera.

"Can you see me on that thing, Officer Singleton? I need the whole world to see how handsome I am." Detail stated as he posed for the camera that wasn't recording.

"The world can see you now, Detail," Ava replied laughing.

Lo and behold, Detail was still riding his bicycle equipped with dirty wash rags and buckets. However, he was in good spirits and had been washing a few vehicles a day trying to get back on his feet. Sgt. Fitzpatrick stopped by the gas station to task Ava with working a residential service complaint. The neighborhood watch reported they were having issues with speeding, stop sign violations, and burglaries at a community meeting. While conducting surveillance, she observed a higher end black sports utility vehicle circling around the neighborhood. The vehicle alone costed more than the houses in this part of town. What was an $80,000.00 car doing in a neighborhood where the average house costs $20,000.00? Ava sat with her eyebrow raised.

She wanted to conduct a traffic stop if they made any violations, but the holding calls of service took priority. Ava responded to a couple of domestic disputes, shopliftings, and vehicle crashes. Once the call load subsided, she returned to the residential area. The same high end black sports utility vehicle drove past. Ava ran the tag and learned the driver had a suspended driver's license.

She keyed up on the radio, "Car 2-4-6, I will be 10-38." The dispatcher seemingly busy watching the news didn't respond.

Ava repeated herself, "Car 2-4-6, I will be 10-38."

Communications copied after apologizing for an operator change.

"2600 Meadow Court out with North Carolina Registration Bravo-Alpha-Charlie-X-X-X-X on a black sports utility vehicle occupied by two.

"Copy," communications advised.

Ava activated her Body Worn Camera and approached the vehicle. The driver was identified as Reggie Thomas, and the passenger was Arthur Perkins.

Reggie stated, "Officer, I'm not going to lie to you. This isn't my car, and I don't have a license. I'm just trying to take my sick friend here to the hospital."

"Well, how long have you been trying to take your friend to the hospital? It's funny because I saw this same exact vehicle riding around earlier, circling the south side." Ava asked in a sarcastic tone, knowing she had caught the men in a lie.

"Ma'am I was looking for someone to drive me to the hospital. This is my car and I have a suspended license. I promise you, I am trying to get some medical assistance. I have shingles," Mr. Perkins spoke up. Lifting his shirt up to show Ava an array of fluid filled blisters around his waistline.

"I also have H-I-V," Mr. Perkins whispered.

Ava felt like the wind had been knocked out of her. Regaining her composure, she collected the men's identification cards, and returned to her patrol vehicle. A background check determined Mr. Perkins had an outstanding warrant for simple possession of marijuana and a history of assaulting law enforcement officers. Ava begin to weigh the pros and cons. Technically, they were supposed to take everyone who had a warrant to jail and keep the camera on until the traffic stop was complete. However, this day was an exception to the rule. Ava deactivated her camera.

"Mr. Perkins, you have a warrant you need to go take care of. I'm going to use my discretion and allow you to seek medical assistance. Now, I cannot guarantee that you will not be stopped again. Neither one of you have a valid driver's license, so I can't tell you to drive legally. However, I am not going to sit here and babysit you. Have a nice day."

The men thanked Ava as she walked back to her car. She had heard plenty of excuses in the past to try to get out of a traffic ticket.

"I'm so sorry officer, I have an uncontrollable bladder."

"My kids just called and said they heard someone breaking in."

"I think my wife is going into labor."

"I'm friends with the chief; wait till I tell him this story."

Mr. Perkins had an award-winning performance. Ava knew that was one of those situations that she should just keep to herself. The service complaint was a fight for another day. She prayed that her Sergeant wouldn't pick that video to watch. However, in her mind losing a job that pays $17.00 an hour versus potentially assisting in the well-being of someone living with H-I-V was a risk she was willing to take. Ava now saw firsthand the disadvantages of the cameras. With the implementation of body worn cameras, it appeared to her that more people were going to jail. Officers could no longer cut breaks without facing scrutiny from the public and constant monitoring from supervisors. Get out of jail free cards were given out sparingly, unlike in the pre-camera age.

Eventually, body worn cameras had become the norm. With so much going on in society, it almost seemed that an officer's testimony was no good in a courtroom unless the incident was recorded on camera. Ava received a notice of case assignment from the District Attorney's Office. She looked up the case report and learned Xavier Cooper was to stand trial for the aggravated assault of Santiago Ruiz. A subpoena soon followed, considering Ava had the best video footage out of all the responding officers.

Ava went to Superior Court, a step above the jungle zoo downstairs at District Court. After about four hours of playing the waiting game, the District Attorney emerged and apologized to Ava, as the court was still doing jury selection. Ava had no qualms with just sitting in the courtroom getting paid time and a half. Besides, she was halfway entertained watching the tedious process of jury selection.

The District Attorney asked all the potential jurors, "Have you ever been involved in a situation with the police that may make you biased to the officer's testimony? Are you okay with the fact that the victim was potentially under the influence of marijuana? Have you heard anything in the media about this case?"

The Defense Attorney asked the potential jurors, "Have you ever been a victim of a crime? Can you think of anything about the nature of this case that may make it difficult for you to examine the issues at hand in a completely fair and impartial manner without prejudice?

The juror selection was becoming painful. One potential juror stated, "Man, I don't really fool with the police like that. I have been arrested before, and I was completely wrong for having that weed on me. I just didn't like how the situation went down, you feel me?"

Another potential juror stated, "I am pro-police. I have a long line of family that are part of the Blue Line. Whatever the officers say happened, I believe."

The jurors had finally been selected three hours later. Ava placed her left hand on the Bible and her right hand in the air as she swore to tell the truth, the whole truth, and nothing but the truth, so help her God.

The District Attorney began, "Were you at 9121 Piedmont Garden the night in question?"

"Yes, I was," Ava replied.

"Why were you out there so early in the morning?" The District Attorney asked making eye contact with the jurors.

"I responded to assist with a shooting," Ava didn't want to say too much and leave room for an attack by the defense attorney.

"What can you tell me about the shooting, Officer Singleton?"

"The victim, Mr. Ruiz reported that he had been outside waiting on a friend to purchase wrestling tickets. While waiting, "Swag-B," an associate from high school, stopped by with some friends to see if he wanted to rap. After a short encounter, Mr. Ruiz was lured to the back of Swag-B's vehicle. There he was robbed at gunpoint and shot while attempting to run away." Ava replied looking at the jurors.

"Did Mr. Ruiz appear to be under the influence of marijuana, Officer Singleton?" The District Attorney asked with her hands on her hips.

"Yes, there was a strong odor of marijuana emanating from his person. Furthermore, he had red eyes and dilated pupils. Mr. Ruiz admitted to smoking marijuana, and a bong was in the middle of the crime scene."

"Is this the video footage that you recorded, Officer Singleton?"

"Yes, it is." Ava advised, squinting at the 32" television.

The District Attorney began to play Ava's body worn camera footage for the judge and jurors. The video began with Ava driving into the neighborhood with her blue lights illuminating. She then entered the residence where Mr. Ruiz was laying on the couch receiving first aid from officers. It was obvious that Mr. Ruiz was in pain.

Mr. Ruiz repeatedly asked Ava, "Am I going to die?"

Mr. Ruiz had thirteen family members inside the residence panicking. The camera picked up great audio and visual accounts of the incident. It even had Ava clearly regurgitating Mr. Ruiz's account of events. Ava took notice to her insensitive tone of voice while the video played. She was in need of a vacation; the daily foolery encountered during a police day was taking its toll.

Ava was allowed to step down out of the hot seat at the end of the video. Thankfully, the Defense Attorney didn't have any questions for her and didn't allow his client to take the stand. However, Mr. Ruiz did take the stand. He had cut his long curly hair and exchanged his bad boy wardrobe for a professional appearance.

"Mr. Ruiz, can you recount the events the evening you were shot, for the court please? The District Attorney asked.

"Yes, sir. I was at my parent's house waiting on my friend Ba Tu. We were going to pick up some wrestling tickets from one of his friends. Then it all happened. Swag-B dropped by the house with an old friend from High School. I thought it was a little bit disrespectful that he showed up at my parent's house. So, I asked Swag B, "What are you doing man? This is my parent's house!" Swag-B said, "Man, I came through to see if you were trying to rap." Then I headed to Swag B's car. Next thing you know, two people jumped out the car and robbed me at gunpoint. They told me to get down on my knees and made me cover my face with my t-shirt. I could feel the butt of the gun at the back of my head. The other two guys were going through my pockets. They stole $30.00 and a ounce of weed from me. I begged them to let me go. Someone punched me and I took off running in the house. I heard a couple of gunshots on the way inside. Once I got in the house, I realized I was shot in my gluteus maximus."

"Do you see Swag-B in the courtroom today? If so, please point him out." The District Attorney directed.

"He right there," Mr. Ruiz pointed to Mr. Cooper.

It was time for the defense attorney's line of questioning.

"How often do you smoke marijuana Mr. Ruiz?"

"About seven times a week." Mr. Ruiz replied without hesitation.

"Basically, you smoke marijuana every single day?"

"Yes, I do." Mr. Ruiz advised nodding his head yes.

"How can you possibly point at my client and accuse him of being Swag-B, when you admit to being a drug user?!"

"Dude, I do smoke weed. However, I attend college and hold down a full-time job."

"Would your full-time job consist of being a drug dealer? I see where you have been convicted of Possession with Intent to Sell and Deliver Marijuana, Simple Possession of Marijuana, and Drug Paraphernalia." The defense attorney asked trying to ruin Mr. Ruiz's credibility.

"I am not a drug dealer. I simply buy my weed like I buy my groceries, in extra bulk." The jurors giggled.

"Order in the courtroom!" The judge yelled, hitting his mallet.

"Mr. Ruiz, did my client hold a gun to your head and rob you?"

"Yes, they made me cover my face and get on my knees. Your client was there and didn't do anything to stop it. He drove to my house with two thugs. He set me up. I had never seen the other two guys before."

It was finally time for closing arguments.

The District Attorney faced the jurors, "Yes, Mr. Ruiz had marijuana in his system the night he was robbed and shot. However, the last six presidents of the United States of America admitted to smoking marijuana. The fact that they had smoked marijuana did not hinder them from running a country. My client was shot and robbed at gun point. Mr. Cooper, better known as Swag-B, had every intention to cause harm to my client. He was more involved in this incident than OJ, and the glove fits."

The Defense Attorney began talking in a calm tone, "What we have here is a big misunderstanding. Mr. Ruiz was so drunk and high, he got his rap lyrics confused with reality. Mr. Ruiz doesn't know who did what to him. My client was simply at the wrong place at the wrong time. This young man does not deserve to spend any time in jail over a crime the state has failed to prove without a shadow of doubt."

After deliberations, Mr. Cooper was found guilty of Assault Inflicting Serious Injury to the ASS-ets and Robbery with a Dangerous Weapon. He had no place in the streets if he was willing to shoot and kill someone over $30.00. Ava understood that without her body worn camera, justice might not have prevailed in the courtroom.

CHAPTER 10

THE COME UP

Ava had successfully completed an advancement examination that would provide her the opportunity to leave patrol. This was against the advice of a few white male officers who advised Ava to stay in patrol. She was unsure if those officers were afraid of a black woman with a high potential of being promoted or if they truly wanted her to understand the duties of a patrol officer before moving up the ranks. Nonetheless, Ava was raised to advance herself at each given opportunity. A new Street Crimes Unit was being implemented to monitor violent offenders and reduce crime in the Criminal Investigation Division. Without thought, Ava applied for the plain clothes detective position by submitting a transfer request up the chain of command. By mid-March, Ava completed the Street Crimes Written Examination.

The first question read, "What sets you apart from the other candidates?"

Ava elaborated on her educational background, policing experience, street smarts, and the color of her skin. Not only could the sister be dropped off in a high crime area, she could blend in with the community that raised her, and testify in a court of law to articulate facts. Ava didn't hold anything back, reiterating her training and experience throughout the written examination.

The stars were lining up for Ava career-wise, but something was still missing. She was completely single, the possibility of becoming the forty-year old woman living with cats was a highly probable scenario with each passing day. Sgt. Fitzpatrick approved Ava for a day off to attend her sorority sister's wedding in Virginia Beach. Ava made the road trip with her soror Everly, the crazy "Tre." The trip consisted of cold fried chicken, 90's R&B, girl talk, and the latest updates of Everly's love life. Hell, we know Ava's love life was non-existent. Her last date was planned around the city bus schedule, being that the young man had no ride. Embarrassed, Ava figured she should keep that one a secret, especially since she had to play cabby to get him back home.

They arrived at the rooftop wedding which exuded a theme of simplistic elegance. Ava's twenty-three sorority sisters sat together wearing their red sundresses under the perfect summer sun. God delivered a nice flowing breeze so the ladies didn't have to worry about perspiring. Glancing back a row behind her, Ava noticed that same welcomed breeze was also disrespecting one of her sorority sister's weave. When Ava turned back around eye contact was made with a young man. She gave him a little smile as he was directed to sit closer to the bride's family. Ava thought to herself, Damn, that light skin man is handsome, has a good grade of hair, and knows how to rock a bowtie.

Ava redirected her energy and focused on the wedding ceremony. The bride and groom poured two different bottles of sand into one vase signifying they were now a unit. Next, they prematurely tongued each other down before the officiant could say the words, "You may now kiss the bride." During cocktail hour Ava indulged in shrimp cocktail, crab dip, and fresh fruit. The sorority sisters entered the reception hall together only to learn that there was assigned seating.

Ava hoped that the young man she made eye contact with earlier would be assigned to her table. She started looking for table number 23 and realized that she couldn't have been that lucky. The young man was sitting approximately four tables away with her sorority sister, Jada. Then it happened again. Across the dinner table their eyes crossed paths.

"Girl, he is so cute," Ava whispered to Everly.

"Who are you talking about?"

"Look at the light skin guy wearing that blue sports coat, bow tie, and khaki dress pants to your 6 o'clock." Everly discretely caught a glance of the young man.

Ava pulled out her smart phone and texted Jada: "Does he have a ring on his finger?"

Jada took it upon herself to interview the young man named Nigel. A name that should have meant simple country folk.

"So, Nigel what do you do?"

"I'm currently in Dental School back east."

"Are you single?" Jada asked sternly, knowing men lie and their definition of single varies.

"Yes, single and ready to mingle?" Nigel replied energetically.

"Do you have any kids?" Jada knew that was a deal breaker for Ava.

"Yeah, I have one. No, I'm kidding. I would like a child once I am married though."

"Are you looking for a wife?" Another sorority sister butted in.

"Yes, I am actually at that point in my life. It is time to settle down." Nigel could feel the heat coming from the sorority sisters.

"Are you down with meeting someone?"

"I certainly am."

Jada escorted Nigel to Ava's table and introduced the two. Ava had an empty seat to her right compliments of someone named Jerimiah not showing up.

"Would you like to take a seat?" Ava asked in an inviting tone.

"Of course," Nigel replied adjusting his bow tie.

Jada went back to her table and watched from afar. Nigel and Ava hit it off very well. They both had goofy personalities and were complete science geeks with degrees in Biology. Nigel left the table briefly to use the restroom.

"Girl, he got some sense. I like him already." Everly told Ava.

"We will see. I'm not sure if he is feeling me." Ava stated, not wanting to play herself.

Nigel returned to the table and they enjoyed salmon smothered in a light lemon butter sauce, plated over a bed of sautéed spinach, and creamy garlic mashed potatoes. Ava had so many butterflies in her stomach that she could hardly eat. Instead, she just kept smiling into Nigel's eyes.

The bride and groom enjoyed their first dance together. Afterwards, the DJ dropped the beat and many people began to hit the dance floor.

"Would you like to step outside for a moment?" Nigel asked.

Ava played along but didn't want to stray far away. Many hopeless romantics have one-night stands after weddings. She didn't want to be in that boat of jump off girls who get drowned and never crowned with a ring.

"Can I have your phone number? I would love to take you out to lunch sometime during my fall break?" Nigel stated stumbling over his words.

Without hesitation Ava gave up her digits. They continued talking outside just passing the time. She nearly missed the tradition of the sorority sisters singing to the bride. Everly quickly realized Ava was missing and alerted her. Ava walked inside the reception hall followed by Nigel. The wedding attendees laughed as Ava joined the circle. She was walking at such a fast pace that when it was time to sing she was out of breath. Ava motioned the words "apples" and "oranges" with a huge smile.

The DJ started the party back up with some Hip-Hop. Then the DJ switched up the beat playing, "Let's Stay Together" by Al Green.

"This is it. Our song is playing." Nigel took Ava by the hand escorting her to the dance floor.

Ava was nervous with her novice dance skills but knew her form fitting dress would give her a few brownie points. Agni had helped Ava master a simple two-step for her senior prom. Ava maintained the movements in her arsenal, slowly moving her feet, and swaying. Nigel was trying to move in closer but was unsure where to place his hands, being a true gentleman and all. The sorority sisters watched them dancing like it was a movie matinee. Nigel's aunt noticed the chemistry between the two and began taking photographs.

Jada told Ava, "Girl, oh my gosh! You all are equally yoked. I actually believe he stole one or two of your dance moves." Jada was laughing uncontrollably when Ava stepped off the dance floor.

Next thing you know, Nigel introduced Ava to his aunt and father. It was a relief to know that he came from a loving family that was trying to marry him off with the quickness. So much for waiting to meet the parents.

Ava and Everly drove back home in a rainstorm after saying their goodbyes.

"Girl, you done came down here to this wedding and found your husband."

"Hush your mouth. I wonder how long it will take for him to hit me up?" Ava knew that if he texted the same day he was interested in an official relationship. Now if he waited a few days, then he was just likely looking for a friend with benefits.

When the clock struck 2300 hours, Ava received a text from Nigel: "Hey beautiful, just wanted to see if you made it home safely."

The text confirmed Ava had made a lasting impression on the future dentist. Back at work, she received an invitation to interview for the Street Crimes Detective position. Ava was now balancing her career and a blossoming long-distance love life. When October rolled around, Nigel asked Ava to join him at the Minor Hills Haunted Farms. The farm had several different activities from hay rides to haunted slaughter houses. The thought of a haunted date made Ava's stomach turn, knowing she had an uncontrollable bladder. She forced herself to use the restroom before they began participating in the activities. Ava wasn't going to risk having any accidents. They walked into the pitch-black slaughter house and came to a complete stop.

"Ava, I think I better go to my car...I have a little flashlight. I can't see anything." Nigel whispered.

"You scared, huh?" Ava whispered with a New Orleans drawl. In her mind the flashlight wasn't a bad idea, but she wanted to secretly test Nigel's manhood.

"Come on, let's do it. Forget that light." Nigel replied gently reaching for Ava's hand. Inside Nigel was squirming.

Monsters, clowns, and zombies were popping out of every corner. Luckily, they were unable to touch the patrons. The two worked extremely well together, clearing corners to make it out safely. Ava enjoyed the hay ride, minus the zombies jumping on back of the trailer with loud heavy metal chainsaws. As the ride was ending, Nigel pulled Ava in closer to kiss her soft moist lips. Ava consented to the advance and sparks began to fly. Sadly, the two had to hit the road which was an untimely ending to their budding romance.

In the upcoming weeks, Nigel was extremely attentive and supportive in Ava's career advancement pursuits. He managed to chisel some time out of his own busy schedule to help Ava prepare for her interview, thanks to Skype and FaceTime. Deep down, Ava didn't want to be a patrol cop dating a future dentist. Her current job title just didn't seem to pack a big enough punch next to his. However, the idea of being a sexy detective dating a future dentist was far more appealing. The morning of the interview, Ava received a text message of encouragement from Nigel: "The best way to predict your future is to create it."

After a short meditation, Ava dropped down to her knees before the slightest inkling of doubt had a chance to creep in. She refused to allow the devil to play tricks on her mind and began reciting the "Serenity Prayer." Ava had already professed the position was hers.

While sitting in the waiting room of the Police Plaza, Ava focused on her breathing, two deep breaths in followed by two deep breaths out.

A Lieutenant walked by, "They will be with you in a moment; good luck, Singleton."

"Thank you, sir." Ava replied still focusing on her breathing. A minute later the conference door opened.

The Captain asked, "Are you ready? Just relax okay."

"Yes sir, I'm ready as I will ever be."

Ava walked into the room amongst several high-ranking officers with a lot of brass. The brass was simply extra metal given to officers who had been promoted. There was a Corporal, Sergeant, Lieutenant, and Captain seated at the table. The roundtable interview began.

"How are you going to connect with people in the community?" Lieutenant inquired.

"I understand that there is great tension between the police and community in today's world. Fortunately, I am highly personable and can talk to people by simply finding common ground. I treat all people with respect which has led me to make various connections with members of the community from diverse backgrounds." Ava responded maintaining her composure.

"What was your toughest interview?" The Captain asked in an interrogative tone.

"Well I interviewed a sexual assault victim that was forced to perform oral sex at gunpoint during a home invasion. She was hesitant to allow the nurse to collect an oral swab. I calmly explained to the victim that she was indeed a victim and that the Minor Hills's Police Department was going to do everything in our power to bring her justice. In fact, my brothers and sisters in law enforcement were risking their lives at that very moment, engaging in a vehicle pursuit of the suspects. My fellow officers were able to track her cell phone that had been stolen during the robbery. Ultimately, I was able to convince the victim to submit to an oral swab which led to a twenty-year sentence for her attacker." Ava answered knowing that the Captain had sent her accolades on that particular report, hoping it would be an example for the entire police department.

The Sergeant was next, "What can you tell me about Miranda Rights?"

Pausing for a second to repeat the question in her head Ava replied, "I read Miranda Rights when I wish to question someone under arrest or in my custody. I'm very familiar with constitutional law. Also, if someone has been detained for a significant amount of time, I read them their Miranda Rights to be on the safe side. I know how defense attorneys play dirty." The interview panel appeared to be impressed with the response.

"What was your biggest mistake in your career?" The Corporal asked.

"Once, I had a young man confess to having a firearm and being a felon on a traffic stop. Unfortunately, my body worn camera was inoperable at the time. So, I had to take a chance and re-interview him, hoping that he would confess again. Thankfully it all worked out. Today, if it didn't happen on camera, then it didn't happen."

"This is the hardest question of the day... Is there anything else that you would like to tell us?" The Captain stated grinning.

Showing all her pearly whites, Ava replied, "Well of course, I would like to say that I am a hard worker. Given the opportunity to be a Street Crimes Unit Detective, I could further cultivate my investigative skills and be a valuable team player. Thank you again for the opportunity and I look forward to hearing from you all soon."

Ava stood up from her seat and shook everyone's hand firmly.

A day later the Sergeant called to say, "Welcome to Street Crimes, Detective Singleton."

"Thank you, sir."

"We fought for you. Are you excited?"

"Yes, I was just trying to spare you from listening to my high-pitched voice screaming." Ava replied giggling.

When she finished talking to the Sergeant, Ava loudly announced, "Detective Singleton in the HOUSE!"

Grandma Rose who had dropped off some collard greens started shouting, "Praise the Lord!"

Agni broke out in a cheer, "Go Ava! Go Ava! Go! When can you start?! Yeah! Yeah! DE-TECT-IVE! Yeah! Yeah!"

The family celebrated over a few draft beers at the local bar. Afterwards a flirtatious Ava called Nigel, "Detective Singleton speaking, this call is regarding an ongoing investigation. My report says you've been a bad boy."

"Please come arrest me, Detective. I'm so proud of you! I knew you would get the position." Nigel replied ecstatically.

"Yes, God is good," Ava proclaimed.

"So, Detective after you book me, may I have the pleasure of taking you out? I know this really good gourmet burger joint in Raleigh." Nigel knew Ava was a big girl at heart.

"I will check my schedule, but I'm sure Detective Singleton always has time for you." Ava joked.

The two met up enjoying monster burgers and college football on the big screen television. During halftime, Ava and Nigel began eye-balling the milkshake menu. The two couldn't resist sharing a milk chocolate milkshake with extra whip cream and a cherry on top. Ava enjoyed doing the simple things with Nigel because she knew he was balling on a budget with excessive student loans.

After the game, Nigel walked Ava to her car and began talking.

"I have never felt this way before. This is different. You have all the qualities that are on my checklist. You are educated, kind-spirited, beautiful, and not crazy...Ava Elise Singleton, will you be my girlfriend?"

Ava paused for a minute. Had she finally met the right guy? The man that she had been impatiently waiting for. Nigel was not like the other clowns in her past who could've very easily been named JailATM Needing Money Azz, Down Low Creeping Azz, Look Good from the Outside but No Brain Having Azz, and Whole Family on the Side Lying Azz.

"Yes, because you have met the requirements on my checklist. You are God-fearing, child-free, educated, and don't have a criminal record...Oh, you know I had to check." Ava shrugged her shoulders innocently.

Nigel grabbed Ava's hand and looked into her eyes, "I hope you enjoyed your last day being single."

Ava immediately felt winded, knowing she had found her Boaz. The man she had been praying for every night. In a week's time, Ava had a man, received a promotion at work, and a stranger had even paid for her lunch one day. *Ezekial 34:26, "I will make them and the places all around My hill a blessing; and I will cause showers to come down in their season; there shall be showers of blessings."* Detective Singleton was surely feeling blessed and it finally appeared to be her season.

CHAPTER 11

DETECTIVE SINGLETON

On the first of April, the new Street Crimes Unit (SCU) began a week-long training. They were brought up to speed on gang intelligence, report writing, and how to properly handle confidential informants. Ava's new squad consisted of all males. There was a Sergeant, Corporal, and four other detectives. The squad hit the ground running, as the command staff was receiving pressure from city council to reduce violent offenses in the city.

Intelligence had been gathered that Linwood Reavis was hiding out at the Central Motel operating a green Lexus. Mr. Reavis was wanted for Robbery, Kidnapping, and Assault with a Deadly Weapon. His bond was preset at half a million dollars by a superior court judge.

Ava loaded up her police gear into an undercover gold minivan with her new partner, Detective Everhart. The van had a soccer ball sticker on the rear bumper that provided the illusion of a soccer mom mobile versus a police car. Everhart's skin matched that of a Hershey Chocolate bar, he stood 6'5, weighing 210 pounds, with a bald-head, and athletic-build. Ava quickly learned that Everhart always made time for his family. Like clockwork at 2000 hours, he would call his children and they would recite the Lord's prayer before bed. Ava knew firsthand plenty of officers who put so much into work that they neglected their families.

Ava sat in the backseat adjusting her binoculars while Everhart parked the van. Ava began to focus on the target room 145. The Sergeant parked on the eastside while the other two detectives positioned west of the motel. Ava's first stake out was appearing to be without event. She was sitting in a cold van, with no heat running, and a growling stomach. Not to mention her bladder was full and four hours had passed with no signs of the wanted suspect.

The Sergeant keyed up on the radio, "So does anyone have a plan to lure Mr. Reavis out his room?"

"How about we get the front desk to call his room and tell him to pick up a package?" Ava suggested.

The Sergeant didn't totally dismiss the idea, however playing devil's advocate, he presented a counter argument. "What if he doesn't pick up his package immediately?" The comment caused crickets on the radio.

"So, Ava... Do you feel comfortable pretending to hit his Lexus with the minivan and knocking on the door? Once the target exits the room, the rest of the squad will come out and help effect an arrest."

"Yes, that's fine," Ava replied confident in her acting abilities.

After all, she had performed in a couple of high school plays and even received a standing ovation after delivering her monologue. Switching seats, Everhart locked and loaded his long gun.

"Everhart, the signal confirming the target is me pulling my ponytail," Ava demonstrated.

"I got you, Singleton," Everhart spoke levelheadedly.

Ava took a deep breath and pulled the minivan very close to the suspect's car. At first, Ava thought she accidently hit the damn thing because it appeared the vehicles were touching. She stepped out of the van looking for "pretend damage," hoping to cause a scene. Ava staggered to the front door like a drunk, giving the common two knocks on the door. The loud obnoxious police knock would have been a dead giveaway. She heard footsteps coming to the door. A man fitting the description of Mr. Reavis opened the door.

Ava slowly pulled her ponytail, "Sorry to bother you. Is that car yours? I accidently hit it. Look I'm going to be honest, I don't have any money… but we can work something out."

"Damn! Let me finish putting my clothes on." The man replied.

Ava walked back out to the vehicles looking at the non-existent damage. Mr. Reavis joined shortly after.

"Is that new or old damage?" Ava asked, pulling her ponytail while pointing at the passenger door of the Lexus.

The sound of the minivan doors opening behind her brought a sense of relief. Everhart jumped out the back seat with his long gun, forcing Mr. Reavis to drop down to his knees with his hands on his head. A miscommunication had the other members of the squad still approaching on foot. Ava quickly switched gears from acting to placing Mr. Reavis in handcuffs. He was transported to jail without incident. The Street Crimes Unit's first operation was successful due to Ava's Oscar Award winning performance and Detective Everhart's keen observation.

This was only the beginning in reducing violent offenses in Minor Hills. A few hours later, the Street Crimes Unit was tasked with apprehending Brice Rogers. The unit understood they needed to continue proving themselves amongst the community and the command staff. Mr. Rogers was a white male, mid-twenties, 6'0 tall, medium build with a buzz cut. He was last seen wearing khaki overalls and a white t-shirt. He gave the local pharmacy a full surprise when he stepped into the building.

"How may I help you sir?" The pharmacy technician asked.

Mr. Rogers replied, "I need to pick up my Xanax pills. My name is Brice Rogers; birthdate February 6th, 1995."

"I'm sorry sir, but I don't see that prescription on file."

"Well see this, bitch!" Mr. Rogers screamed pulling out a revolver.

Mr. Rogers proceeded to jump over the counter, stealing $7,000.00 in prescription medication, before fleeing on foot. His mother called after watching the six o'clock news, fearful of her drug addicted son. She notified emergency communications that he was currently asleep on her couch. The Street Crimes Squad loaded up in the soccer mom mobile and the Sergeant's old sports utility vehicle.

The house was in a neighborhood where street lights were non-existent. The mailbox numbers were hard to read and deer were roaming freely on the backroads.

"Okay guys, the house should be up the street. Let's park short and approach on foot. The mom left the front and back door unlocked for us." The Sergeant reported to the squad.

"I hate to be the bearer of bad news Serge, but it looks like we are parked right in front of the house." Ava replied laughing.

"Damn it! Corporal take the back in case he runs out. Everyone else stack up from the front of the house." The Sergeant quickly ordered.

Ava got in the middle of the stack with Becker in front of her. Becker was a hella attractive, muscular white man, standing over 6 feet tall with a cowboy's vibe. Ava often wondered how it would be to ride his rodeo. On the other hand, Cohen a short, sloppy, dip-spitting mess was behind her with his holey jeans.

Peeking into the window she observed Mr. Rogers laid out on the couch.

"Minor Hills Police! Let me see your hands!" The squad yelled running through the front door.

A startled Mr. Rogers fell to the ground, "Shit, man you got me." He mumbled in a dazed voice.

Ava and Everhart cuffed Mr. Rogers as the rest of the squad conducted a protective frisk of the residence. The arrest was broadcasted over the 11 o'clock news highlighting the benefits of the Street Crimes Unit.

Unfortunately, the positive press was short-lived like a celebrity marriage. Minor Hills Police Department was back under scrutiny, after a news article reported that more African American motorists were stopped for traffic violations than any other ethnicity. Reports from traffic stops proved there was a disproportionate ratio of African American motorists being searched compared to white motorists. Lastly, the article shed light on police officers finding more guns and drugs on African American motorists.

The Chief immediately put out a Special Order in response to the racial disparity allegations releasing the following statement to the media:

"Minor Hill's police officers will no longer initiate traffic stops for minor traffic infractions. I will be having an independent study completed by experts at several universities to gain an understanding on why racial disparities are present in our community. Furthermore, all members of the police department will be undergoing mandatory sensitivity training on racial disparities."

The Police Union called an emergency meeting at the clubhouse to discuss the Special Order. Ava had been a part of the union since police academy. The union had plenty of benefits which included an attorney, access to the gun range, a monthly box of ammo, and most enticingly a $50,000.00 retirement bonus check. Ava had never been to an actual meeting though. However, her new Sergeant used his stripes to voluntarily force the squad to attend the meeting. The clubhouse was packed with officers standing along the wall because the chairs quickly filled. The age of officers in the room ranged from twenty-one to fifty-five. There were officers from all ethnicities present. The Sergeant at Arms called the meeting to order, "We usually only have five members present, but send out an email that says "EMERGENCY" in the subject line and we get a full house. I'm glad everyone is here today. The union speaker is currently working on a statement to release to the media. Our police attorney will be here tonight for a limited time due to a prior engagement. Let's address questions to our attorney first. This is an open forum."

A young white narcotics detective stood to his feet, "Can the Chief legally tell us that we can't stop for minor traffic infractions? We swore to enforce the laws of this state under oath."

"Yes, the Chief can. Traffic infractions are not criminal matters. There is nothing criminal about having a broken taillight. Do I agree with the way the Chief is going about this? Absolutely not!" The attorney responded.

An older white male officer stood to his feet rubbing his beer belly, "I think that we should stop even more cars in the city, despite the special order. Let's show them what we are made of!" Ava sat quietly thinking that was a horrible idea.

"As the police union attorney, I want you all to be aware that you could be subject to termination for failing to obey the Special Order."

Ava was slightly uncomfortable knowing she took an oath of office to better serve her community, not work for a department that wouldn't stand up and confront allegations of racism. She believed the older officer was coming from a "good old boy mentality." Who was the "them" he was referring to?

In Minor Hills, there was more violence in predominantly black neighborhoods. To be more specific, there were 45 reported homicides last year; 43 of the 45 homicides occurred in black neighborhoods. It didn't take a rocket scientist to figure out that patrol officers should spend more time in those areas to reduce crime. Ava saw the benefit of stopping cars in high crime areas to reduce crime.

She knew that having highly visible marked police cars in high crime areas was positive. Stopping cars did not necessarily equate to issuing traffic citations for minor violations. Officers could take time during the traffic stop to build community partnerships, learning more about the issues affecting the neighborhoods they serve and protect. The officer also had discretion to give verbal warnings.

A female training officer voiced concern, "Several recruits in the 36th Police Basic Introductory Academy put in resignation letters this week. They decided to work for other police agencies because of the racial allegations. We are having a hard time keeping good quality candidates here." She flopped down in her seat.

Leduc asked, "How can we let our community know that we are not a bunch of racist officers?"

"Why don't we give the public access to our body worn cameras? This way our community can see firsthand that we are a transparent agency." Ava asked with her squad in agreeance.

"That is a great idea, but it could be an invasion of privacy showing camera footage of someone's house to the public without their permission," The attorney explained with a smile. Ava quickly realized how being transparent could be problematic.

Someone in the crowd boldly yelled out, "Is it true that the Chief said he would not let the city burn down over one officer? Even if the officer was completely justified in their action."

The attorney paused briefly, "Yes, it's true. The Chief would be willing to sacrifice an officer. I learned this in a closed-door meeting after the incident in Missouri."

The police meeting ended on a sour note to say the least. Officers returned to work fearful of losing their job for conducting traffic stops. The special order didn't really affect the Street Crime Detectives who were given more leeway. They were ordered to properly document the target logs of the violent offenders in case they had to stop a violent offender for a minor infraction.

In other news, Ava and Nigel were going strong like *Romeo and Juliet*. The two flew to California so Nigel could present his research at a dental conference. Ava felt so rejuvenated, having a man striving to create a future for himself through hard work and commitment. These were old-fashioned values rarely found in men her age.

The two were full of surprises for each other. Ava secretly got tickets to attend a live taping of *Jimmy Kimmel*. After the show, Nigel took Ava on a couple's night Hollywood Tour. The two gazed at the Pacific Ocean and celebrity mansions from afar as the dry Cali heat caressed their skin. The next day, they celebrated their five-month anniversary at a fine Korean BBQ restaurant. Ava was hesitant to try new cuisine, but a glass of Korean rice wine eased her mind. Every woman likes a man that expands her horizons. They shared a variety of exquisite meats which included bulgogi (marinated beef), prime galbi (short ribs), and samgyubsal (pork belly). Nigel had a little pre-dessert dish that consisted of assorted flavored macaroons.

However, Ava was his main dessert that night. A naturally rich chocolate cake baked and prepped to perfection. Nigel started off with a slight tease that consisted of light kisses in between her inner thighs. Then he began to lick every letter of the alphabet on her vagina. Ava's cake was moist and decadent. He nibbled up Ava's stomach to her chocolate drop nipples. Proceeding with light kisses on the neck until their eyes meet. Nigel looked deep into Ava's soul. Deciding not to be greedy, the remainder of dessert was saran wrapped and saved for later, as they barely held on to their Christian morals.

CHAPTER 12

CRACKED BLACK & BLUE

Ava returned home to North Carolina, embracing the devilish humidity. She sensed more violence erupting in the city, knowing the heat brings out the worst in people. The gang members were wearing their bandanas and posting various emoji adorned comments on social media. The comments were the usual, "Pull up on us! We out here nigga! The gas in hit my line!" The girlfriend of a prominent gang member even posted, "My pussy must be made in China because I got Great Walls!" Funny thing was, Ava had recently been tasked with strip searching that same female, who had a gun located in her waistband, and crack hidden inside her pussy cat. It was hard not to pass judgement on the lost soul.

The Street Crimes Squad filed into the conference room.

"Okay guys, there was a homicide at 1300 hours at the Minor Hills Square Apartments. The victim, Mr. Walters was killed instantly after taking buckshot rounds to the neck from a 20-gauge shotgun in broad daylight. The sun beamed over his lifeless body for nearly an hour before the police were called." Sergeant reported.

"So where do we come into play?" Cohen asked.

"Damn, Cohen! Can I finish? The suspect, Tavion Staton's cell phone is being tracked by the Violent Criminal Apprehension Team. If they get a ping in Minor Hills we will be assisting." The Sergeant stated before stepping out of the conference room.

"Guys, I received a phone call coming into work. Apparently, the victim and suspect grew up together in a rough city up north. The young men moved down here for a fresh start at life, but they couldn't put their past life behind them. This is all over a verbal altercation on who was going to keep the stolen gun." Ava updated the squad after receiving a call from Lynn.

"Who told you?" Becker asked.

Ava giggled, "I can't release my sources."

The Sergeant walked back into the conference room, "Load up! The phone is pinging at Turk St. Singleton, Cohen, and I will ride together to be the jump out vehicle. Everhart and Becker, drive separately so we have additional cars to tail the suspect." Ava was relieved to get a break from Everhart who was officially her "work husband." The two would bicker about the air condition and radio every night. Not to mention, every other day Everhart was giving Ava crap about her driving, tactics, and officer safety preferences.

The Street Crimes Squad headed to the area equipped with their Level III tactical vest and thigh rig holsters. The information for the phone was coming in slower than usual. The ping was showing the suspects phone near the bus station and apartment complex. Ava notified the bus station's security to be on the lookout for the suspect.

"Latest hit…the vehicle is now traveling westbound on Maple St.," A detective with the Violent Criminal Apprehension Team advised.

"I'm on Maple St. Got a city bus that just made a stop at 6th street." Everhart stated.

Cohen replied, "Hey we are coming your way, man!"

"Got a black male fitting the description of Mr. Staton exiting the bus. Looks like he just entered a white hatchback," Everhart keyed up frazzled. The detectives scrambled to get to his location.

Ava was riding in the front right passenger seat waiting on Cohen to hit the gas before a killer left town. Cohen's driving reminded Ava of a senior citizen needing their license privileges revoked.

The Sergeant was also growing impatient with Cohen's driving, "Damn son, hit the gas! Go through the red light!"

"Oh! My bad," Cohen replied while spitting out tobacco dip into an empty soda bottle.

Adrenaline began to run through Ava's veins. The mere thought of Mr. Staton killing a "friend" in broad daylight made her mentally prepare for a shootout.

"Looks like the vehicle just dropped off an occupant. I believe the target is still in the vehicle. I can't continue to follow them or they will recognize me. Where are you guys?" Everhart asked impatiently.

"We're with you," Sergeant replied.

Cohen finally stepped on the gas passing the hatchback.

"Suspect is ducked down, peeking out the back-left passenger window. Let's get ready for a vehicle take down." Ava stated, confirming the suspect with a quick glance.

"On my count. One…Two…Go." Becker stated, getting ahead of himself.

Becker bumped the rear, Cohen stopped in front abruptly, and Everhart blocked in the hatchback instantaneously. The Street Crimes Detectives successfully extracted all occupants without incident, including Mr. Staton. Cohen was so excited that Ava was scared to look down. She knew he likely had a "hard on."

"We just arrested a murder suspect aren't you excited?" Cohen asked Ava.

"This is what we are supposed to do." Ava replied in a nonchalant voice.

She was more than willing to help assist in getting a murder suspect off the street. However, the fact two young black men had just lost their lives was nothing to be excited about. One mother had to deal with a son who no longer had a heartbeat, while the other would watch her son rot in an overcrowded prison system.

Ava caught a ride back to the office with Everhart to complete some paperwork.

"So, Singleton, you know how I've been moody lately?" Everhart asked.

"No, I didn't notice your daily pettiness." Ava replied sarcastically.

"Shut up! I get like this every time. My wife's pregnant."

"Congratulations! It makes sense; I've been dealing with the pregnant bougie version of Everhart." Ava couldn't resist the extra commentary.

"I'm thinking about applying for a daytime position inside the Criminal Investigation Division. You know working Monday through Friday would allow me to see my children grow up."

"I think that is a good move. Remember, everyone told us not to stay on Street Crimes for a long time anyway. Just use it as a stepping stone. Look, if you leave, I'm leaving too."

"Yeah, I have to do what is best for my family first."

"I understand that. Well, I found out Nigel doesn't sleep at night when I'm at work. I think it will give him a peace of mind if I had a desk job too."

"When he finishes residency you're going to be a housewife Singleton." Everhart snickered.

"I'm sure I will be working somewhere. Just in case he bumps his head one day. I know how the male brain works now."

At approximately 2000 hours the SCU began conducting surveillance at the Minor Hills Suites Room 221. Intelligence had been received from a homicide detective that "Marsalis" was at the location. Marsalis was responsible for a gang shooting that left two injured and three killed. Ava and Everhart were still riding around together in the soccer mom mobile. On this night, it was Ava's turn to drive. She parked north of Broad St. with an unobstructed view of the target location. The Sergeant and Corporal were together in the unmarked sports utility vehicle on the southern side. Becker and Cohen were parked in an unmarked truck covering the western entrance.

Multiple vehicles were circling the hotel parking lot honking their horns. This was slightly suspicious activity. Considering most people just call each other on their cell phones, send text messages, or utilize the old school method of exerting themselves physically by knocking on the door. An uncanny feeling came over Ava and Everhart. Ava updated other members of the Street Crimes Squad on the tactical communication channel.

"Hey guys…Cars keep driving through the parking lot beeping their horns at the target location."

"Just got word it might be a retaliation shooting from a confidential informant." The Sergeant replied. Things were readily apparent, Ava hypothesized they were trying to lure the suspect out of the room for "street justice."

Twenty minutes prior, Ava and Everhart had been sitting in the parking lot. They grabbed a copy of the hotel registry to confirm they were watching the correct hotel room and to find out exactly how many rooms were occupied. Disturbingly, Ava observed children playing in the parking lot of the drug-infested hotel.

"So, do we have a plan in case they start shooting out here?" Ava asked concerned.

"We are going to be relieved by the Violent Fugitive Apprehension Team at 0500 hours. Give me a second, Singleton." The Sergeant replied.

A few minutes later, the Sergeant gave out orders, "Everhart and Singleton, you render aid on the parking lot if they start shooting. Becker and Cohen, stop any cars leaving the western entrance. Corporal and I will stop vehicles leaving out the southern entrance."

The squad acknowledged the Sergeant personally who made rounds delivering pizza to everyone's post. The plan lacked so much detail that it was merely a preliminary rough draft. Anxious, Ava laid back in the driver's seat and secretly released a silent fart.

In the rearview mirror, she observed Everhart looking around to see if something spilled or needed to be thrown out of the van.

Everhart asked with his face scrunched up, "Do you smell that, Singleton?"

"Excuse me," Ava replied modestly before bursting out in laughter.

"Damn, Singleton that is awful; you should be ashamed of yourself. Has Nigel smelled one of those before? You smell like a baby's diaper!" Everhart ranted, putting Ava in a jovial mood.

There was little to no activity at the hotel room, so Ava gave Nigel a call. Maintaining a positive line of communication was essential in a long-distance relationship. It wasn't easy considering Ava worked from 1600 hours to 0300 hours, four nights on four nights off. Nigel was still on his school schedule of 0800 hours to 1700 hours, Monday through Friday.

"Hey Lady... How's your night going?" Nigel answered the phone after a single ring.

"Good...Just wanted to give you a quick call while I had the chance."

Everhart could be heard in the background, "Nigel, tell her to be more confident! Oh…and to stop passing gas!" Ava gave the phone to Everhart so he could stop yelling.

Everhart wanted Ava to embrace her new role through leadership and be more assertive with the other (white) detectives. Ava felt like she could be direct with Everhart because he was married to a strong black woman and could relate. Naturally, Ava was more reserved with the other detectives. She didn't want to be labeled the "Angry Black Woman" throughout the department. Being a strong educated black woman with an ear to the streets was intimating to testosterone driven men. A lot of times, Ava could predict problems before they ever occurred. More often than not, she would place bets with Everhart unannounced to the squad.

"Man, I wanted to tell you, a young Commercial Property Detective was inquiring about Ava's love life. I shut that down for you and let him know she is practically married." A gossiping Everhart continued.

"Thanks Bro, good looking out." Nigel replied.

"Aye…The little murderers are coming out the room. Did you want to talk to Ava?" Everhart passed the phone to Ava urgently.

"Goodnight…I've got to go." Ava told Nigel abruptly.

"Stay safe out there tonight."

It was nearing midnight when five black males exited room 221. They were wearing dark black clothing with hoodies over their head. Ava used her binoculars to see the males were conducting counter surveillance, by looking over their shoulders and checking their surroundings. A few of the males were making furtive movements reaching inside their pants. The street savvy side of Ava knew they were likely gripping guns. Not to be judgmental, she allowed room for the small possibility they might be checking their manhood. None of the males had taken notice of Ava's minivan, parked approximately one hundred yards away.

Ava keyed up on the radio to update the squad, "Five black males walking southwest towards the horseshoe portion of the parking lot. They are entering a red PT cruiser and a pearl Chrysler 300. On the move...looks like they are heading southbound on the Interstate."

"Copy. Everhart and Singleton, maintain visual of the target location. We will follow the vehicles." Sergeant stated.

The two cars went through the drive thru of a fast food spot. Unable to positively identify Marsalis, the detectives doing mobile surveillance returned to their perspective positions. Ava knew it was hard for white people to positively identify black people and vice versa.

Nearly thirty minutes later, Ava observed a silver sedan pull up and park between rooms 221 and 223. The driver was Ashleigh Keys, a twenty-year-old white female with blatantly obvious breast implants. She was accompanied by a young black male and female dressed in red. Ms. Keys was none other than Marsalis' girlfriend.

The same black males that had left Room 221 earlier were walking back with food in hand. However, the two cars they left in were not visible from Ava's position. She relayed the message to the squad being that Everhart's radio was dying. Looking through her binoculars, Ava observed the group of individuals going in and out of rooms 221 and 223.

Ava keyed up on the radio, "Hey guys, a dark colored Mustang just stopped parallel to rooms 221 and 223."

Before Ava could complete her sentence, "Pop! Pop! Pop!" was heard in the background. The initial noise sounded like fireworks.

"Shots fired! The Mustang is shooting! They are shooting back! Someone advise main dispatch now!" Ava screamed over the radio shocked.

"Copy. Let me know when the vehicles leave." Sergeant advised with active gunfire in the background.

"Let's go!" Everhart yelled at Ava.

Ava activated her subpar emergency lights and siren. Once the gunfire ceased Ava entered the parking lot to render aid. Ava's left hand was on the steering wheel and her right hand was on the Glock. She had unholstered her weapon from her thigh rig. Everhart was in the back of the van with his riffle loaded.

"Pop! Pop!" A second exchange of gunfire began.

"Move! They are shooting at us Ava!" Everhart yelled.

"Scrrrrrrrr! Boom!" Ava crashed into the target's hotel room. The suspects took off running on foot and entered vehicles.

"Signal 0 at the Minor Hills Suites! Officer Down! Two cars leaving the scene and several suspects running on foot. Send me everything you have." Everhart blurted out over Ava's radio on main dispatch.

"Need EMS emergency traffic, officer down with multiple gunshot wounds." Everhart advised.

"Ava, stay with me! Stay with me! Damn it!" Everhart panicked watching Ava bloody and unresponsive.

Meanwhile, Sergeant and Corporal were in a short vehicle pursuit with the Mustang. Every window had been shot out including the front windshield.

Corporal rolled down his passenger window and shouted at the driver, "Go ahead and stop the car, Mother Fucker!" The supervisors were driving right beside the Mustang that was continuing to slow roll.

The driver known on the street as ".357," was observed throwing a copious amount of marijuana outside the driver's window. The passenger jumped out of the vehicle and fled the area before ".357" stopped the car.

Becker and Cohen were busy with the Chrysler 300 they stopped on the Interstate.

Cohen keyed up on the radio, "Be advised vehicle occupied six times."

Communications copied.

"Go ahead and start paramedics emergency traffic. We have a male suffering from multiple gunshot wounds." Cohen continued.

"Paramedics en-route."

Becker screamed, "Start us some more cars! Don't fucking move!" Becker and Cohen held the occupants at gunpoint.

Escaping the chaos, Everhart rushed to Agni's house to deliver the news personally. It took him a long three minutes of sitting in the car staring blankly at Agni's front door, just mentally preparing to muster up enough courage and strength. Finally, he was able to relay the horrible message to Agni about her daughter, his "work wife."

"Ma'am I'm so sorry, but there has been a bad accident. I need you to come with me." Everhart stated unable to hold back the tears. Agni actually had to console Everhart before he escorted her to the hospital.

Agni went to the information desk inside the Emergency Room. "I need to see my daughter, Ava Elise Singleton."

"I'm sorry ma'am this hospital is on lockdown." The secretary advised.

"Okay." Agni replied nonchalantly prior to unexpectedly bolting through the secured facility. She wasn't going to let any man or woman stop her from seeing her daughter.

Everhart stepped outside to call Nigel. "Hey man this is Everhart. How fast can you get here? Ava's been hurt!